1

The Hillbilly Bible

John

By
Stevie Rey

Stevie Rey Contact Information:
hillbillybible@gmail.com

Original Cover Art by Jo Naylor.
Back Cover Photo by Kendra Rey.

Thankees

Thankee Kindly to my sweet, darlin' wife that believed in me when nobody else did. I love ye, Sunshine.

Thankee Kindly to my Daddies. The one down here that taught me to fear God. And the one up yonder whose grace my fears allayed.

Thankee Kindly to my momma who always stood by us and took care a me when I was sick and could'n take care a myself.

Lastly, Thankee Kindly to the wunnerful, wunnerful folks on Myspace, especially the lovely and creative Jo fer my cover art. This would'n a happened were it not fer y'all.

Ferword

HiDee Y'all!
This here's Stevie Rey. Thankee kindly fer buyin' The Hillbilly Bible.
I shore do 'preciate it and my bill collectors 'preciate it too!

I just wanna say one thang. Y'all, please, please, please don't use this
as a study Bible! They's a whole bunch a real smart fellers and Bible
scholars and theologs and what not that's done writ many a good study
Bible. I ain't one of 'em! I know a little Greek and a little Hebrew.
One of 'em owns a liquor store and one of 'em owns a laudromat!
HEE-HAW!!!

This here's kindly fer fun, kindly to give folks some insight into the
heart of the good Lord, and kindly to interduce folks to Jesus that ain't
never read no Bible before. Mostly fer that last one, cuz I reckon we
ort to be tellin' folks and such.

It ain't no word fer word translation, more of a paraphrase, that there's
edgy-cated talk fer *I kindly put it in my own words*. I tried not to add
ner take away from it y'all, but I reckon I could be wrong 'bout some
stuff, so's I ask y'all and the good Lord to fergive me on the front end.

Now, to be sure, some folks ain't gonna like this nary a bit. Y'all
fergive me too. I'm a tryin' to tell folks 'bout Jesus that ain't a gonna
read no regular Bible. I know this here's way out on the edge, y'all.
But sometimes reckon ye got to go out to the edge a the boat to grab
folks that's overboard?

But if'n ye wanna do some serious study, y'ort to go buy yeself one a
them there high falutin' Bibles, what with the purdy maps and charts
and pitchers and what not. Thank y'all from the bottom a my heart! I
hope ye enjoy The Hillbilly Bible.

THIS HERE IS GOOD NEWS! SPREAD IT LIKE PEANUT
BUTTER, Y'ALL!!!

In the Love a King Jesus,
Stevie Rey

Surely you are one of them, for your
accent gives you away.
- Matthew 26:73 [NIV]

Way back yonder at the start a things was the Word, and the Word was right there with God, and sure 'nuff, He was God, y'all. He was right there with God from the very start. Ever'thang was made by 'eem and wud'n nuthin' made that He did'n make. In 'eem was life, and that there life was just a shinin' fer folks to see ri-cheer in this darkness, but folks did'n even understand.

A Feller Hollarin' in the Country

Now, there was a feller that come from God, and 'ees name was John. That there feller come to tell folks 'bout this shinin' light so that ever'body could believe in 'eem. He wud'n this here light hisownself, but he come to tell folks 'bout the light. The light that shines on ever'body had up and come right into this here world.

He come up into the world, but even though He made ever'thang, we did'n even pay 'eem no mind. He come to see 'ees

7

folks, but we did'n let 'eem in. But the ones that did let 'eem in, and put their trust in 'eem, he let 'em just up and become sons a God. Young 'uns not born the usual way with mommas and daddys, but born a God. And this here Word become a man and lived ri-cheer with us fer a spell. We seen how shiny He was, the shine a the only son the good Lord ever had, full a grace and truth.

Now, John told folks 'bout 'eem and commenced to hollarin' "This here's the one I was talkin' 'bout when I says 'The feller that comes after me really come way before me so's he's better 'n me by a country mile.'" And we just keep on gettin' heapin' helpin's a grace from 'eem. Cuz all the rules 'bout what's right and wrong come by Moses, but grace and truth come by King Jesus. Ain't nunna us ever seen God, but we seen this here Son a God, so now we kindly know what God's like.

Now, this here's what John told 'em when the religious folk come a callin' to see who he was. He told 'em straight up, "I ain't the King yer lookin' fer."

And they asked 'eem, "Well then who are ye? Are ye Elijah?"

And he says, "I shore ain't."

And they says, "Reckon yer The Prophet?"

8

"Nope" he said.

Then they says, "Well, who are ye? So's we can go and tell on ye to the fellers that sent us. What do ye have to say fer yerself?"

Then John commenced to preachin' from Isaiah "I'm a feller hollarin' in the country, y'all step aside and make way cuz the Lord is a comin'."

And the religious folk says, "How come ye commenced to Baptizin' folks if'n ye ain't the Messiah, ner Elijah, ner The Prophet."

And John spoke up sayin' "I dunk folks with water, but there's a feller standin' ri-cheer amongst us that y'all don't know, and He's 'bout to plumb steal the show, and I ain't even fit to shine 'ees shoes." All this stuff was done over yonder past the Jordan in Bethany where John had commenced to dunkin' folks.

The day after all that stuff happened John saw Jesus comin' and just up and says "Ladies and gentleman, I wont' ye to meet the lamb a God, come to tote off the sin a the whole world! This here's the feller I was talkin' 'bout when I says 'The feller that comes after me really come way before me, so he's better 'n me by a country mile'. I did'n even know this here feller, but 'ee's the reason I come a dunkin' folks in water in the first place."

Then John told 'em straight up "I seen the Spirit drop down outta the sky and light on that there feller somethin' like a dove and I did'n even know 'eem but the good Lord had done already told me to commence to dunkin' folks in this here water and when ye see the Spirit drop down outta the sky and light on a feller, yer gonna know sure 'nuff that's the one that's gonna soon be dunkin' folks in the Holy Spirit. And that is exactly what I seen, y'all, and I'm tellin' ye, sure nuff', that feller there is the Son a God."

Y'alls fixin'to See Some Stuff that'll Turn ye Kettle White

The day after that there happened, John and two a his disciples was hangin' out and when Jesus come a strollin' by John hollered out, "Look Y'all, it's the lamb a God!" And when them two fellers heard it, they come after Jesus. Jesus looked around and saw 'em and says, "Reckon what ch'all hankerin' fer?"

They answered up, "Teacher, where ye livin' at?"

"Come m'on and see", He says. So, around ten or so in the mornin', them two fellers went after 'eem and saw where he was a livin' and just kindly hung out with 'eem all day.

One a these here fellers was Andrew, Simon Rocky's brother. First thing he done was to find ole Rocky and say, "We done found us the promised King", and took 'eem over to see Jesus. When Jesus saw 'eem he says, "Yer Simon, John's boy. But I'm gon' nickname ye Rocky."

The day after that stuff happened, Jesus went over yonder to Galilee and found Philip and says, "Come m'on!" Now Philip come from Bethsaida, same as Andrew and Rocky. Philip hunted up Nathaneal and says, "We done found the feller Moses and the Prophets wrote about in the Bible, Jesus from Nazareth, Joseph's boy."

"I reckon nuthin" any count ever come from Nazareth.", says Nathaneal.

And Philip says "Come see fer yerself, feller."

Jesus saw ole Nathaneal comin' and says, "Look here y'all. Meet ye a real live Israelite. What ye see is what ye get with this feller!."

And Nathanael asked "Do I know ye?"

Jesus answered "I was a watchin' ye under that fig tree when Phillip come and got ye."

And Nathanael says, "Well, sure 'nuff, I reckon ye are the Son a God, and the King a Israel too!"

Jesus answered up, "Ye got all that from me seeing ye under the fig tree? Y'alls fixin' to see some stuff that'll turn ye kettle white." And, he says, "Sure 'nuff, y'all are fixin' to see heaven open up and angels just a runnin' to and fro bringin' me messages."

He Commenced to Shinin' and They Was Plumb Hooked

The day after that stuff happened, Jesus' momma went to a weddin' over yonder at Cana, in Galilee, and Jesus and 'ees disciples was invited too. After while, they run outta wine, and Jesus' momma says to 'eem, "They's outta wine."

"Hun, I don't know what in the world that has to do with me, cuz it ain't time fer me yet."

Then Jesus' momma says to the hired folk, "Just do what He tells ye to."

Now, there was some big ole pots that the Jewish folk used to rinch their hands off in, and they could hold 'bout twenty or thirty gallons. Jesus says to 'em, "Fill them there water pots up all the way, y'all." And they filled 'em til they was 'bout to gush over. Then he told 'em, "Git some a that there and take it over yonder to the weddin' planner." They took it over there, and when the weddin' planner drunk some, he did'n know where it come from, but the hired help knowed it. Then he hollered over to the bridegroom to come 'ere, and says, "Most folks put out the good wine first, and then when folks is kindly tipsy, haul out the cheap stuff, but y'all done saved the best 'til last." That was the first miracle he done, over yonder in Cana, and He commenced to shinin' and the disciples was plumb hooked. After that, he went on back to Capernaum with 'ees momma and brothers and disciples and stayed fer a spell.

This Here's God's House, Not the Flea Market!

When it come time fer the Passover, Jesus went over yonder to Jerusalem. At the temple there was a bunch a fellers sellin' doves and sheep and cattle and such and they was some that was kindly rippin' folks off too. So, Jesus just up and made 'eem a whip outta cords and such and commenced to pitchin' a big fit and whippin' 'em and run ever'body off and dumped out their money. And he says to 'em "Git this mess outta here, this here's God's house, not the flea market!" Later on, 'ees disciples 'membered that it says in the good book, "I'm so crazy 'bout God's house, I'm liable to act like I done lost my mind."

13

Then the Jews says to 'eem, "Who made ye sheriff? Y'ort to up and do a big miracle or somethin' to prove yer somebody in charge."

Jesus answered up, "Ah ight. Tear down this here temple and I'll rebuild it in three days."

And the Jews says "Ye got to be outta yer ever lovin' mind, this here temple took forty six years to build and ye reckon ye can do it in three days?" But what Jesus was really talkin' 'bout was 'ees own body. After he come back to life, we remembered what He said and believed it and ever'thang the good book says 'bout 'eem too. Because a all the miracles he done in Jerusalem a whole mess a folks reckoned He was really the King that was supposed to be comin'. Jesus did'n pay 'em too much mind though, cuz He knowed human nature and how fickle folks can be sometimes.

Fer The Good Lord Commenced to Hankerin' after The World

One night this religious big wig, Nicodemus, come a callin' on Jesus. "Teacher, we reckon God must a sent ye, on account a all the miracles ye done."

Jesus answered up, "Sure 'nuff, ye cain't see the Kingdom a God, less'n ye get reborn."

14

"How in tarnation is a old feller s'posed to git reborn?" says Nicodemus. "He sure 'nuff cain't climb back in 'ees momma's belly and come back out!"

Jesus answered up, "I'm a tellin' it to ye straight here feller, nobody gets into the Kingdom a God, less'n they's born with water and then with the Spirit. Momma's and Daddy's can only make little human babies, but the Holy Spirit makes sons and daughters a God. So don't have a cow 'bout what I just said. The wind commences to blowin' and ye cain't tell if it's a comin' or a goin'. It's kindly like that with folks born a the spirit."

Nicodemus said, "Do what?"

And Jesus says, "You mean to tell me one a the high-falutin' teachers a Israel don't already know this stuff? Sure 'nuff, we's talkin' 'bout stuff we know cuz we seen it, and y'all still don't believe us. If I done told ye 'bout ever'day stuff and ye don't believe, reckon how ye gonna believe if I commence to talkin' 'bout stuff I done seen in heaven? Cuz look here, nobody's ever been to heaven, 'cept yers truly, The Son a Man. And just like Ole Moses toted that serpent up when they was a wanderin' in the country, I gotta be toted up too. So's whoever commences to believin' ort not die, but live ferever. 'Fer the good Lord commenced to hankerin' after the world something fierce, and up and gave 'ees only boy so's whoever took a notion to believe in 'eem ort not die, but just keep on livin' with 'eem in heaven ferever n' ever. Cuz God did'n send me down here to round y'all up and herd ye to hell, he sent me down here to save y'all. The one's that believe in me, ain't gonna get herded to hell, but the one's that don't believe is already cruisin' fer a bruisin' cuz they did'n believe in God's one and only boy.

This here's how I see it. Light come up into the world but folks did'n wanna have nuthin' to do with it, cuz they was misbehavin'. Folks that are misbehavin' and doin' wrong don't want no light to shine on 'em while their doin' it, cuz everybody'll see what they's doin'. But the feller that is really a huntin' fer the truth, comes on into the light so ever'body can look and see that God's done brung 'eem on home.

He's Just a Brimmin' Over With God's Spirit

After that, Jesus and 'ees followers went off into the country in Judea and stayed fer a spell and dunked folks. John was a dunkin' folks too over yonder in Aenon, near Salim, cuz they was a bunch a water there and folks just flocked to 'eem to be dunked. That was

16

before they thowed 'eem in Jail. Then there come a question twixt John's disciples and some Jews 'bout dunkin'. They come over to John and says, "Teacher, that feller that was with ye over yonder on the other side a the Jordan that ye told us 'bout is dunkin' folks and ever'body has commenced to goin' over yonder to get dunked by 'eem."

John says, "I reckon a feller can only git what heaven decides to give 'eem. Y'all heard me say I wud'n King, that I was a gonna kindly interduce 'eem. These folks that's goin' to 'eem, they belong to him, not me, and I'm doggone glad they's a goin' cuz he's the bridegroom and he's come to claim 'ees bride. It's time fer me to step aside and let 'eem have her, y'all.

The feller that comes from up yonder in heaven is King. The feller that comes from down here on earth tells 'bout earthly stuff, but that feller that comes from up yonder is the real King. He tells 'bout heavenly stuff, but folks don't buy it much. The feller that does buy it gives it 'ees stamp of approval. The one that God sent up in here, speaks God's words, cuz He's just a brimmin' over with God's Spirit. The Daddy loves 'ees boy and just up and gave 'eem ever'thang to do as He sees fit. Anybody that puts their trust in that there Son a God is gonna live forever. Anybody that don't believe is a goner, cuz they sins are still on 'em and cain't no sin come up in heaven, God is obliged to destroy it.

When the religious folk heard that Jesus was dunkin' more folks that John (Jesus did'n really do the dunkin', the disciples did), the good Lord up and left Judea and come on back to Galilee.

The Fields Is Ripe Fer The Pickin'

Now, the Good Lord had to cut through Samaria. He come to a town called Sychar, over yonder near the land that Jacob give to 'ees boy Joseph. Jacob's ole well was there, and the good Lord up and had 'eem a little rest cuz he was wore slap out from all that walkin'. I reckon it was 'bout noon.

By and by, a Samaritan woman come to get some water, and Jesus says to her, "Can I git me a drank? (the disciples had gone over yonder to town to get some vittles). Then she up and says, "What in the world are ye talkin' 'bout mister? Y'all Jews cain't have nuthin' to do with us Samaritans", (cuz sure nuff, Jews wud'n sposed to even talk to Samaritans, much less a woman Samaritan!).

Jesus answered up, "Hun, if'n ye knew who ye was talkin' to, you'd be the one askin' fer livin' water, and I'd give it ye, sure 'nuff!"

18

Then she says, "Mister, ye don't even have no bucket, and that there well is a deep 'un, reckon how ye gonna get this here livin' water? Next yer gonna tell me yer better than Abraham that give us this well, and drunk from it way back yonder, with 'ees kin folk and critters."

And Jesus answered up, "Hun, folks that drinks this here water's gonna be thirsty again, but the feller that drinks my water ain't never gonna be thirsty again, but there's a creek gonna run through 'eem that leads right up to the good life."

And that there woman just up and says, "Gimme some a that there water, so's I don't have to come back to this here well ever'day!"

Jesus answered up, "Ah ight then, run and tell yer husband and come on back." And the woman says, "Ain't got no husband."

Jesus says, "Ye sure said a mouthful! Y'aint got one, but-chee did'n mention ye done had five of 'em and y'aint even married to the feller yer livin' with now."

"Mister, I reckon yer one a them there preacher types. So answer me this. Why do y'all Jews say that Jerusalem is the only place ye can go to worship, and us Samaritans say it's ri-cheer at Mount Gerizim, where our kin folk worshipped.

19

Jesus answered up, "Sure 'nuff hun, times a comin' when it won't matter where ye go to worship, whether it be ri-cheer or Jerusalem. Y'all Samaritans don't know a whole lot 'bout praisin' God, but we Jews know all 'bout it, 'cuz we's the chosen folk. But, the times a comin', in fact I reckon it's already here, when folks is gonna praise God in spirit and truth. Yer daddy in heaven is lookin' fer folks that will praise 'eem that way. 'Cuz God is spirit, so folks got to praise 'eem in spirit and truth."

That there woman says, "I reckon The King's a comin'- the one folks call the Christ. When he gets here, he'll teach us all 'bout it."

Then Jesus just up and says, "Yer lookin' at 'eem!"

Round 'bout that time, the disciples come back and 'bout had a cow that He was talkin' to a woman, but none of 'em knowed what they was talkin' 'bout or why. The woman just up and left her jar right there and went back and commenced to blabbin' it to ever'body, "Y'all come 'ere and meet this feller that knowed ever'thang I ever done! Y'all reckon this is the King?" So, the folks just come out in droves to see 'eem.

'Bout that time, the disciples commenced to naggin' on 'eem, "Teacher, come on and get ye some dinner." But he answered up, "I got vittles that y'all don't even know 'bout."

"Reckon who brought 'eem vittles", they asked one 'nuther. Then Jesus taught 'em fer a spell.

"Ya see, my vittles come from doin' what God wants me to do, and from gettin' the job done that he sent me to do. Y'all say "In four more months gon' be time to pick the crops", but look all around ye at the fields, they's already white and ripe fer the pickin'. Y'all know that sayin' "One er 'nuther plants, and one er 'nuther picks", well, sure 'nuff that there's a true story. I have sent ye to pick what ye did'n plant, other folks have done all the sweatin', and y'all are gonna come right in and do the pickin'."

Many a them Samaritan folk commenced to believin' cuz a what that there woman says 'bout "he knew ever'thang I ever did!" When they come out to see him they commenced to naggin' on 'eem to stay fer a spell, so he stayed fer a couple a days, which was 'bout long enough fer 'em to hear what he had to say and believe. Then they says to that there woman, "Now we believe cuz we heard 'eem fer ourselves, not just cuz a what-chee said. Sure 'nuff, he's the Savior a

the world, ah ight."

King Jesus Heals a High Falutin' Feller's Boy

After he stayed with those folks fer a couple a days, He come

on back to Galilee. He'd done said, "A preacher gits respect

ever'where, but 'ees home town." The Galilean folks was glad to see

'eem, cuz they had been at the Passover shindig in Jerusalem and saw

'eem do a bunch a miracles. On 'ees way, he come through Cana

again, where he done that miracle with the wine, and they was a big

shot government big feller over there who's boy was real sick. He had

heard that Jesus had come from Judea and was back in Galilee, so's he

went over to Cana. He hunt up Jesus and commenced to beggin' 'eem

to come back to Capernaum and heal his boy, who was kindly at

death's door.

Jesus answered up, "Y'all ain't fixin'to believe less'n ye see a

bunch a miracles are ye?"

And the feller answered, "Lord, please won't ye come right

now, before he dies." Then Jesus says, "G'on back home now, yer

boy's gonna live."

And the feller believed Jesus and started on back home. When he was on the way, some a his people met 'eem with the news that 'ees boy was doin' a fer sight better. He asked 'em when the boy commenced to feelin' better and they says, "Yesterdee at about one, his fever just up and broke camp." Then it dawned on 'eem that was the same time Jesus had told eem, "Yer boy's gonna live." And that high-falutin' feller and all his kin went to believin' in Jesus. That there was Jesus second big ole miracle that he done in Galilee, onced he'd come on back from Judea.

The Religious Nuts Git Their Drawers in a Bunch

After that, Jesus went on back to Jerusalem cuz they was havin' another one a them there Jewish holy days. Now, over yonder in Jerusalem by the sheep gate, there's this pool called Bethesda, with five high-falutin' porches that's all covered up. All sorts a sick folk- blind, cripples, invalids and what not-used to lay on them there porches. One a them fellers laid out there had been ailin' fer thirty eight years. When Jesus saw 'eem, he knowed how long he'd done been there and up and says, "Reckon ye wanna get well, feller?"

"I cain't , sir", the sick feller says, " cause I ain't got nobody to help me git in yonder pool when the water gits stirred. Ever'time I try, somebody else jumps in their before me."

Jesus told the feller, "Git on up now, git-chee mat, and commence to walkin'!"

'Fore ye could blink that feller was all fixed up! He went on and rolled up 'ees mat and started hoofin' it! But, this here miracle happened on the Sabbath day. So's the religious folk got their drawers in a bunch 'bout it. They hollared at the feller that was a carryin' his mat, "Ye cain't work on the Sabbath day, that's against our laws!"

The man said, "That feller that healed me told me to 'git-chee mat and walk!'"

"The very ideer! Who in tarnation would say that?" they hollared.

The feller did'n know 'cuz Jesus run off into the crowd. But a little later Jesus hunted 'eem up at the Temple and says, "Ah ight, yer well now. Now quit-chee misbehavin' 'fore somethin' worse happens to ye." Then that feller went and blabbed it to the religious big shots that it was Jesus that done the healin'.

So the Jewish religious big shots commenced to givin' Jesus a hard time ever chance they could fer breakin' their Sabbath rules. And Jesus answered up, "Well, I reckon my daddy don't never stop workin' so I ain't fixin' to neither?" Well that really got their dander up and they commenced to tryin' to kill 'eem real hard, cuz He was callin' God 'ees Daddy and that just blew their minds cuz it was kindly puttin' himself on the same level with God. And, he was all the time breakin' their Sabbath rules to boot.

Jesus Tells The Uppity Religious Folk a Thing or Two

Jesus up and told 'em, "Sure 'nuff, y'all, the Son cain't do nuthin' by 'eemself. The Son just does the stuff he sees the Daddy doin'. Cuz the Daddy loves 'ees boy and 'ees done showed 'eem what to do, and the Son's fixin' to do some stuff that'll make healin' this here feller seem plumb piddlin' in comparison. He's fixin' to blow y'alls minds. He's gonna just up and bring dead folks to back to life, just like the Daddy does. And the Daddy's gonna even let the Son be the judge on judgment day, so's ever'body will look up to the Son, same as they look up to the Daddy. And if'n ye don't look up to the Son, ye don't look up to the Daddy neither.

Now, look here y'all. Them folks that's got their ears on and trust God, they's the ones that's got the good life and is gonna keep on livin' ferever. They ain't never gonna get judged fer misbehavin' cuz they done already come into the good life. And I'm tellin' y'all, time's a comin', in fact it's already come, when dead folks is gonna hear me talkin' to 'em, the Son a God talkin', and them that's got their ears on is gonna live! The Daddy is full a life, and He give it to the Son, too. And He's done put the Son in charge a all mankind, cuz 'ees the Son a Man.

Now, don't y'all have a cow 'bout this, 'cuz sure 'nuff the time's a comin' when all dead folks are gonna hear God's boy speak and come on back to life, them that done good to the good life and them that kept on doin' wrong to judgment. But I don't do nary a thang without gettin' with my Daddy. I do what He tells me to do. And when I judge, I judge fair and square, cuz I agree with the Daddy that brung me, I ain't just doin' my own thing.

If'n I was doin' my own thing, what I says would'n hold no water. But somebody else is tellin' folks 'bout me, and sure 'nuff, what he's sayin' is true. As a matter a fack, y'all sent folks to hear ole John the Baptist preach, and he was tellin' it straight. But, the best feller that's talkin' 'bout me ain't no man, but I'm just kindly remindin' y'all 'bout what John says so's ye might just up and believe. John shined fer a spell, and y'all shore did waller in it. But I got somethin' tellin' 'bout me that's better than John, the stuff I done and the stuff I done taught. And the Daddy hisownself has told 'bout me. Y'all ain't never heard ner seen 'eem, and ye ain't took his message to heart cuz ye don't trust me, the feller he sent.

Y'all just pour over the Bible cuz ye think it's gonna give ye the good life, but the Bible talks 'bout me, but ye won't even come to me so's ye can have the good life. Y'all think I care what ye think a me? I don't, cuz I reckon ye don't have God's love up in ye. Fer I come to ye in the name a my Daddy, but ye don't even thow out the welcome mat fer me, but ye'll thow one out fer a feller that's only out fer number one. Taint no wonder y'all won't trust me, cuz yer all too happy to lift up yer buddies, but ye don't care 'bout a feller that comes from God.

But don't get to thinkin' it's me that's gonna drag ye into court before the Daddy. Moses is gonna be the one to do it! Yep, Moses is the feller y'all trust in. But, if ye really trusted Moses, ye'd trust me, cuz Moses told 'bout me in the Bible. And since ye don't believe him, I reckon y'all ain't a gonna believe me neither."

King Jesus Feeds a Whole Mess a Folks

By and by, Jesus crossed on over the Sea a Galilee (some folks call it The Sea a Tiberias). And droves a folks was followin' 'eem ever'where cuz they seen that he was a healin' and doin' mir'cles. Then Jesus come up into the hills and sat a spell with 'ees disciples (now, it was just 'bout time fer the Jewish Passover). After a little bit, Jesus saw all these folks a comin' and turned to Philip and says, "Phillip, reckon how we gone feed all these folks?" He was a givin' Phillip a little quiz, cuz he done already knew what he was fixin' to do.

Phillip hollared out, "I reckon ye'd have to win the lottery to feed all them folks!"

Then ole Andrew, Rocky's brother, chimed in, "There's a little boy over yonder with five little ole loaves a bread and a couple a fish, ye reckon that'll do that trick?"

"Y'all tell ever'body to have a sit", says Jesus.

So all of 'em had a sit right there on the grassy hills and they was five thousand men, not even countin' the women and kids. Then Jesus took them there loaves a bread and says the blessin' and thanked the Lord, and commenced to passin' em out to the folks. And then He done it with the fish too. And they all ate 'til they was full as ticks.

"Now, y'all pick up the leftovers so's nuthin' gets wasted",
Jesus says. Now, they was five loaves to start with, but when we was
done, we had done picked up twelve basket fulls a bread that the folks
could'n even stuff in their bellies! When the folks saw what he'd
done, they got all excited and commenced to wantin' to crown 'eem
King right then and there whether he wanted to or not, sayin' "Ain't no
doubt 'bout it, He's the Prophet we been waitin' fer!" so's he climbed
up further into the hills by 'ees lonesome.

Jesus Come a Strollin' on the Water

That evenin' 'ees disciples come on down to the shore to wait
fer 'eem. It was fixin' to get dark so's they went on ahead and got in
the boat and headed over yonder to Capernaum. 'Fore long it come up
a storm while they was rowin' and they was gettin' tossed around a
good bit. They was three or four miles from shore, when they saw
Jesus just a strollin' on the water comin' after 'em. They commenced
to whoopin' and hollarin somethin' fierce cuz they was plumb skeert
half to death, but Jesus hollared out, "I'm ri-cheer, y'all! Don't be
skeert, now!" Then they just could'n wait to get 'eem in the boat and
'fore ye could snap yer fingers they got where they was goin'.

29

"My Body is Real Vittles"

Come mornin' time, yonder back on the other side a the lake, the folks commenced to crowdin' around lookin' fer Jesus cuz they knowed the disciples went on over and left 'eem there. A bunch a boats from Tiberias come ashore yonder near where He said grace fer the bread and fed all them folks. When they seen Jesus wud'n there and neither was the disciples, they climbed up in their boats and headed over to Capernaum to hunt 'eem up. When they got there, they says, "Rabbi, how in the dickens did ye git over here?"

Jesus answered up, "I reckon truth be told, y'all hunt me up cuz ye was hungry not cuz ye saw a mir'cle. Y'all ort not to pay no mind to stuff that's here today and gone tomorrow like vittles. Y'ort to git up the gumption to find the good life that I can give to ye, cuz that's why God, the Daddy, sent me."

"Reckon what does God want us to do?", they answered.

"This here's the work a God, Just put yer trust in me, the feller he sent", Jesus says.

They answered up, "Now, yer gonna have to show us a real mir'cle 'fore we's gonna put our trust in ye, now whatcha' gonna do? Cuz our kin folk back yonder ate manna whilst they was a hoofin' it in the country, just like the good book says "Moses give 'em bread from up yonder in heaven to chow down on."

Jesus answered up, "Sure 'nuff, it wud'n Moses that give 'em bread, it was my Daddy. And now y'all can have real bread from heaven. The real bread a God is the feller that come down from heaven and offers the good life to ever'body in the world."

"Feller", they says, "pass the bread ever'day from now on."

Jesus says, "I'm the bread a life. If'n a body comes to me, they ain't never gonna be hungry no more. Folks that trust in me ain't gonna be thirsty no more neither. But, y'all ain't trusted in me, even though ye saw me. But, them that the Daddy has give to me is gonna come to me, and I would'n shoo 'em off fer nuthin', no way, no how. Fer I come here from up yonder in heaven to do what God told me to do, not what I took a notion to do myself. And this here is how God wants it, that I ain't gonna lose none a the ones he sends to me, but I'm fixin' to raise all of 'em up at the end a time. Cuz that there's what God wants, that ever'body that looks up to me and trusts in me ort to live ferever in heaven, and I'm fixin' to raise 'em up at the end a time."

Then the folk commenced to flappin' their jaws cuz he says "I'm the bread from up yonder in heaven." They says, "Ain't this here

31

Jesus, Joseph and Mary's boy. Reckon how can he say, 'I come down from up yonder heaven.'"

"Stop flappin' yer jaws, y'all", Jesus says. "Nary a one a ye can come to me, less'n the Daddy reels 'em in, and I sure 'nuff will raise 'em up at the end a time. Just like the good book says, 'They's all gonna be taught by God'. Ever'body that hears what the Daddy is sayin' and learns from 'eem is gonna come to me. Nobody has ever laid eyes on the Daddy 'cept me, that come down from God. Sure nuff, y'all, anybody who trusts in me already has the good life! Yep, I'm the bread a life ah ight. Yer kin folk chowed down on manna in the country, but they all up and died. But, this here bread from up yonder in heaven gives the good life to ever'body that eats. I'm the bread in the flesh, that come from up yonder in heaven. Anybody that eats this here bread is gonna just up and live ferever. This here bread is my very own body that I'm fixin' to give so's the whole wide world can live ferever."

Then they commenced to fussin' with one another, "Reckon how can this here feller give us 'ees body to eat?"

Then Jesus spoke up, "Sure 'nuff, less'n ye eat by body and drink my blood, ye cain't have the good life in ye. But the ones that eats my body and drinks my blood has got the good life, and I'm a gonna raise 'em up at the end a time. Fer my body is real vittles, and my blood is good to drink. Ever'body that eats my body and drinks my blood comes to stay in me and I come to stay in them. Just like my Daddy gives me life, I give it to the folks that feeds on me. I am the real bread come down from up yonder in heaven. Anybody that eats this here bread will live ferever n' ever and not have to die like yer kin folks did when they ate that there Manna." He says all that whilst he was a teachin' folks in the church over yonder at Capernaum.

"Y'all Ain't Fixin' to Leave Me Too Are Ye"

When they heard all that, even the disciples says, "Shewwee, we ain't never heard a such. How can anybody do that?"

Jesus knew they had commenced to mumblin' 'bout it and says, "That 'un got yer goat did'n it? Then what in the world are ye gonna think, when ye see the Son a Man go up yonder to heaven again. It's the Spirit that's gonna give y'all the good life. There ain't nuthin' y'all can do to earn it. What I just says is Spirit words and they is life words. But some a y'all don't believe what I done said. Jesus knew from the get go who did'n trust 'eem and who was fixin' to turn on 'eem. Then he says, "Y'all see what I mean now when I say folks cain't come to me less'n the Daddy reels 'em in?"

This here's when many of 'ees folks turned tail and left 'eem.

"Y'all ain't fixin' to leave me too, are ye?", Jesus says to 'ees twelve disciples.

Rocky says, "Lord, reckon where would we even go? Yer the only feller that tells 'bout how to have the good life. We believe what yer tellin' and we know good and well that yer the Holy One a God."

"Really, it was me that chose y'all, but one a ye is a booger." (He was talkin' 'bout that ole turncoat Judas, Simon Iscariot's boy.)

"Reckon HowHe Knows So Much? He Ain't Got No Schoolin'."

After that, Jesus stayed in Galilee fer a spell, kindly travellin' round twixt all the towns. He decided he might not ort to go over to Judea no more, seein' as how them Jewish religious big shots was a hatchin' a plot to kill 'eem and all. 'Fore long it was time fer the Festival a Tents and Jesus' brothers commenced to naggin' on 'eem to go over yonder to Judea to join in the party. "Y'ort to go where all yer folks can see them mir'cles ye do", they jabbed at 'eem. "Ye cain't be a rock star if'n ye go to hidin'. If'n ye can really do all this mirac'lous

34

stuff, why not take yer show on the road?" Cuz his very own brothers did'n even believe in 'eem.

Jesus answered up. "Now ain't the right time fer me to go. Y'all can go anytime and it don't make no diff'ernce, cuz ever'body ain't commenced to hatin' on y'all. But they's sure 'nuff hatin' on me, cuz I done told 'em they's misbehavin'. Y'all run on and go. I'm a gon' stay fer a spell, cuz it ain't my time yet." So, Jesus stayed fer a spell in Galilee.

But after 'ees brothers come on to the festival, Jesus went on ahead and come too, but he did'n tell nobody. Them ole Jewish religious big shots commenced to huntin' fer 'eem at the festival and askin' around fer 'eem. Folks was just a gossipin' up a storm 'bout 'eem too, some folks says, "He's a right good feller." Others says, "He's a snake oil salesman, leadin' folks astray like he does". But nobody had the gumption to say a good word 'bout 'eem in front a nobody, cuz they was skeert a the religious big shots.

Then, 'bout halfway through the festival, Jesus went up yonder to the Temple and commenced to teachin' folks. The Jewish big shots 'bout had a cow, "Reckon how he knows so much, he ain't got no schoolin'?", they wondered.

Jesus answered up, "I ain't teachin' my own stuff, but God's stuff cuz He's the one that brung me. Anybody who has a hankerin' to do what God wants knows whether my stuff is from God or just from me. Fellers that tell their own stuff is lookin' fer pats on the back from other folks, but the feller that's talkin' up the one that sent 'eem is right and doin' it fer the right reasons too. None a y'all does what Moses tells ye to do! As a matter a fact, ye'd just as soon kill me as look at me!

The crowd answered 'eem, "Yer outta yer ever lovin'mind. Ye got boogers livin' in ye. Ain't nobody tryin' to kill ye!"

"I did some work on the Sabbath by healin' that feller, and that just really got-cher goat", Jesus answered. "But y'all do it too, when ye circumcise little babies like Moses says to do (actually it goes even farther back than that, yer kin folk Abraham used to do it.) cuz if it comes time to circumsize and it's the Sabbath day, ye go right on and do it, so's ye can do what Moses told ye to. So, why in tarnation would ye wanna judge me fer completely healin' a feller on the Sabbath day? Use yer head. Think 'bout it, and ye'll see the good sense in what I'm sayin'."

"If'n Ye Trust Me, Come on and Drink Up!"

Some a the folks that stayed in Jerusalem started talkin' "Ain't that there the feller they's been tryin' to kill? But he's ri-cheer 'fore God and ever'body just a talkin' plain as day, and they ain't doin' nuthin to stop 'eem. Y'all reckon the religious big shots have really started to believe he is The King? But, I don't see how he could be. We know this here feller's home town. When The King comes, he's just gonna pop up outta nowheres. Ain't nobody gonna know where he come from."

When Jesus was a teachin' at the Temple, he hollared out, "Yep, 'sure nuff, y'all know me and ye know my home town. But I speak fer a feller, ye don't know, and he's true blue. I know 'eem cuz I come from 'eem. He's the one that brung me." Then the religious big shots tried to take 'eem to jail, but nobody could touch 'eem, cuz it wud'n time yet.

"Ain't No Prophet Ever Been No Hayseed Hillbilly From Galilee!"

A whole mess a folks that was crowded 'round the Temple believed in 'eem. They says, "Well, I reckon I cain't imagine The King doin' much more mir'cles than this here feller." When the religious big

37

shots started hearin' this kinda talk, they sent the Temple cops after 'eem to thow 'eem in jail. But Jesus just up and says, "I reckon I might stay a little longer, y'all, then I'll be moseyin' back to the feller that sent me. Y'all still be lookin' fer me, but ye won't find me, and ye won't be able to come after me neither."

That made the religious big shots' eyes kindly glaze over. "Where in the world does he think he's gonna go?" they wondered. "Maybe he's gonna up and leave and go talk to Jews in other lands or even folks that ain't Jewish! Wonder what he means when he says, 'Y'all still be lookin' fer me, but ye won't find me, and ye won't be able to come after me neither'."

On the last great day a the festival, Jesus stood up and hollared out, "If y'all are thirsty, I wished ye'd come to me! If'n ye trust me, come on and drink up! Cuz the good book says that creeks a livin' water's gonna flow from inside ye." Now, what He was talkin' 'bout was the Holy Spirit, but folks had'n got The Spirit yet, cuz Jesus ain't gone on to glory yet.

When all the folks heard 'eem say it, they says, "surely this feller is The Prophet." Some other folks was sayin', "Yep, he's The King, ah ight." And some a the other folks was sayin' "He cain't be!

38

Is the Messiah gonna be a hillbilly from Galilee?" cuz the good book teaches plain and simple that The King is gonna be one a David's kin folk, born in Bethlehem, same as King David. So, their was a big ole controversy 'bout 'eem. Some folks won'ted to have 'eem thrown in jail, but nobody laid their paws on 'eem just yet.

The Temple cops that they sent to bust 'eem, run on back to the religious big shots. "Why did'n y'all arrest 'eem?" they asked.

"Look here, we ain't never heard nobody talk like that!", they says.

"Don't tell us ye believe in 'eem, too?" the religious big shots huffed. "Do ye see any a the religious leaders believin' in him? These hayseed crowds from the country don't know nuthin'! They's cursed!

Nicodemus, the feller that had come a callin' on Jesus earlier spoke up, "Does the law allow us to convict a feller 'fore he's done had a fair trial?" he wondered.

"Are ye one a them there hillbilly Galileans too?" they says. "Read yer Bible, ain't no prophet ever been no hayseed hillbilly from Galilee!" Then they all quit meetin' and went on home.

Jesus and the Lady Caught Cheatin'

Jesus went on back to the mount a olives, but bright and early the next mornin' he come on back to the Temple. By and by, a bunch a folks come up and he sat down and commenced to teachin' 'em. Right in the middle of it, the religious teachers come up with a lady they had caught cheatin' and pitched her down right in front a ever'body. "Teacher", they huffed, "we done caught this here lady cheatin'. Moses rules says we ort to chuck rocks at her till she's dead. What do ye have to say 'bout it?"

They was plumb settin' a trap fer 'eem so's they could use 'ees words against 'eem, but Jesus did'n do nuthin' but hunker down and commence to writin' in the dirt. They just kept on naggin' at 'eem so he got up in a minute and says, "Ah ight. Go ahead and kill her. But I won't the feller that ain't never misbehaved none to chuck the first rock." Then he hunkered down and again and commenced to writin' in the dirt.

When they heard that, well, they just up and hoofed it outta there, startin' with the older fellers, 'til there wud'n nobody left amongst all those folk but Jesus and that lady. Then Jesus got up and says, "Hun, where'd all the finger pointers go? Did'n nary a one of 'em stay to chuck rocks?"

"No, Lord", she answered.

And Jesus says, "Then I ain't chuckin' none either. Run on now, and quit-chee misbehavin'."

Jesus Dukes It Out With the Religious Big Shots

Then Jesus spoke to the folks again, "I'm the light a the world. The one that follows me ain't gonna be trippin' 'round in the dark, cuz y'all are gonna have the light to lead ye through life."

The religious teachers answered up, "Yer tellin' lies 'bout yerself!"

Jesus says, "What I'm sayin' stands up, even though I'm sayin' it 'bout myself cuz I know where I come from and I know where I'm a goin'. Y'all don't know nuthin' 'bout me. Y'all are judgin' me the way people tend to judge, but I ain't judgin' nobody. But if'n I did decide to judge somebody, I'd be right in doin it, cuz my judgment ain't just me, it's my daddy that brung me too. Y'alls own teachin's say that if two folks agree on somethin' it's a done deal. Well, ye got one witness- that's me, and ye got another, my Daddy that brung me."

"Reckon where is yer daddy?" they says.

Jesus answered up, "Since ye don't know me, ye don't know my Daddy. If'n ye knew me, ye'd know my Daddy too." Jesus said all this stuff while he was a teachin' in the Temple where they take the offerin', but still the cops didn' come get 'eem, cuz it wud'n time fer 'eem yet. A little later he says, "I'm fixin' to git on outta here. Y'all are gonna come huntin' fer me, but yer still gonna die sinners. Y'all cain't go where I'm goin'."

The religious big shots said, "Reckon what's he gonna do, kill 'eemself? What's he mean, y'all cain't go where I'm goin'."

Then he answered up, "Y'all are from down here. I am from up yonder. Y'all come from this world. I don't. That's why I says y'all are gonna die sinners, cuz unless ye start believin' I am who I say, then yer gonna die sinners."

"Who are ye then? Tell it!" they huffed.

Jesus answered up, "I'm who I been sayin' I am all along. They's a whole lot more I could say 'bout it and a whole lot more I could bust y'all on, but I only say what the one that brung me tells me to say and everything He says is true." But they still did'n git that he was talkin' bout his Daddy in heaven.

Jesus went on to say, "When ye git through totin' the Son a Man up, then y'all are gonna get it and see that I don't do nuthin' without my Daddy, and I tell it like straight like He tells me to. And the feller that brung me is still with me, He ain't gone nowhere, fer I'm always doin' stuff that makes 'eem happy." Many a the folks that heard 'eem say all this stuff trusted it was all true.

Jesus says this to the folks who trusted 'eem, "Y'all are really my disciples if'n ye keep doin' what I say. And y'all are gonna know what's true, and that there truth is gonna set-chee free."

"But we's Abraham's kin folk, we ain't never been no slaves. What'cha mean set free?" they said.

Jesus answered up, "Anybody that misbehaves is a slave to misbehavin'. A slave ain't in the family, but a son is in the family ferever. So, if'n the Son cuts ye loose, yer gonna really be free. I know y'all are Abraham's kin folk. But some a y'all are hankerin' to kill me, cuz y'aint takin' my message to heart. I tell ye stuff that I saw when I was with my Daddy, but y'all do what yer own daddy says."

"Our daddy is Abraham", they says.

"No it ain't" he says "cuz if y'all was Abrahams kids, y'all would be good like he was. I been tellin' it to y'all real straight, just

43

like I heard it from God, but y'all got a mind to kill me. Abraham would'n never do that. Nope. Y'all are doin' what yer real daddy tells ye to, when ye do that."

Then they says, "We ain't the one that's no count daddy is anybody's guess! Our real daddy is the one and only God."

Jesus answered up, "If'n God was yer daddy, ye'd love on me, cuz I come from God. I did'n come here on my own, He brung me. Why are y'all so dimwitted? It's cuz ye cain't understand. Cuz y'all are the devils kids, and ye just cain't wait to do what he's wantin' ye to. He's a killer and has been from the start, and he cain't stand it when folks tell it straight. He ain't even got it in 'eem to tell it straight. When he lies, it just comes natural, cuz he's liar and the father a lies. So, here I am tellin' it straight, so naturally y'all ain't gonna get it. Which a y'all can honestly say ye've seen me misbehave? And if I'm tellin' it straight why don't ye believe what I'm sayin'? Anyone whose Daddy is God will gladly listen to what He has to say. Y'all don't listen, so that there's proof enough that y'all ain't God's young' uns."

The people answered 'eem. "Ye ain't nuthin' but a Samaritan with a booger in 'eem."

Jesus says, "Nope. I ain't got no booger in me. I'm all about givin' the respect to my Daddy. And y'all are all about hackin' on me. I don't really wanna be the man, but if God wants me to be the man, then it's His call. I'm tellin' it straight, y'all. Anybody that does what I tell 'em to, ain't never gonna die!"

Then they says, " Now we know ye got a booger in ye. Abraham and all the ole preachers back yonder in the Bible died, yer sittin' here tellin' us that folks that do what ye say ain't never gonna die! Are ye better than Abraham, cuz he died? Are ye better than all the ole time preachers, cuz they died. Just who do ye think ye are?"

Jesus answered up, "If I'm just braggin' on myself, nobody should pay me no mind. But it's my Daddy that brags on me. Y'all say "He's our God, but y'all don't even know 'eem. But, I know 'eem. If'n I says I did'n I'd be tellin' stretchers too! But, sure 'nuff I know 'eem and I do what he tells me to. Yer great granddaddy, Abraham, saw me comin' and he plumb got excited 'bout it."

And the folks says, "Ye ain't even fifty year old, how ye gone claim ye know Abraham?"

Jesus answered up, "God has been around a lot longer than Abraham." Well, that done it. They picked up rocks to chuck at 'eem and kill 'eem right then. But, Jesus hid from 'em and left the Temple.

Jesus Heals a Blind Feller With Mud Pies
and Ticks Off The Religious Nuts…Again

As Jesus was strollin' along, he eyed a feller that'd been blind all 'ees life. His disciples asked 'eem, "Teacher, why's this feller blind? cuz he misbehaved or cuz his momma and daddy did?"

"It ain't because a his misbehavin' or his momma and daddy's" Jesus says. "It's so's God could do somethin' wonderful fer 'eem. We all got to get goin', doin' what we gotta do to make this thing play out like the feller that brung me wants it to, cuz there ain't much time left 'fore night time, then won't nobody be able to do nuthin'. But as long as I'm here, I reckon I can still spiff this place up a bit."

Then he spat on the dirt and made a little mud pie and put it on that blind fellers eyes. Then he says, "Go over yonder and warsh that off in the pool a Siloam (that means sent, y'all). So he went over yonder and done it and come back seein' plain as day! 'Eees next door neighbors that knowed 'eem as a ole blind bum says, "Y'all reckon

46

that's the same feller? That blind bum?" Some folks says he was and some says, "Naw, that ain't him, but it sure does look like 'eem. But the bum kept on sayin' "It's me, y'all!"

The folks asked 'eem, "How'd ye git healed then?"

He told 'em, "That feller called Jesus made a mud pie and rubbed it on my eyes and says 'Go over yonder and warsh that off in the pool a Siloam' so I done it and now I can see!

"Where did he go?" they asked.

"Don't rightly know" he says.

Then they rounded 'eem up and took 'eem to see the religious big shots. Now, would'n ye know it, he done this here healin' on the Sabbath day. The religious big shots grilled 'eem real good, and he told 'em, "He rubbed mud a pie on my eyeballs and when I warshed it off I could see."

Some a the religious big shots says, "This feller ain't from God. If'n he was he would'n be workin' on the Sabbath." Other folks says, "If'n he's just a run a mill sinner, then how's he doin' such amazin' stuff?" So there was a whole big uproar 'bout it. Then the religious big shots brought the feller in fer a grillin' one more time and huffed, "What do ye have to say 'bout all this? It was yer eyes he opened!"

The man answered, "I reckon he must be a prophet."

The Jewish religious big shots would'n believe that he used to be blind so they called his momma and daddy in fer a grillin' too. They asked 'em, "Is that there yer boy? Has he been blind all 'ees life, and if'n he has, explain how he can see now?"

The fellers parents said, "We know this is our boy, and we know he's been blind all 'ees life, but we don't know how in the world he can see now or who dunnit? He's a grown man. Why don't ye ask him?" They put it this way, cuz they was kindly skeert a the religious big shots, cuz they had done said anybody talkin' 'bout Jesus bein' The King was gonna be put out a the church. That's why they said, 'He's a grown man. Why don't ye ask him?'

So they brought the feller in again fer questioning and says to 'eem "Why don't ye get right with God. We know this feller Jesus ain't nuthin' but a sinner."

"I don't know nuthin' 'bout that" says the feller. But, I do know one thing, "Back yonder I was blind and now I can see."

"How did he do it? How did he heal ye?" they asked.

"Look here!" the feller hollared out. "I done told ye. Are ye deaf? Why do ye got to keep hearin' it? Are y'all fixin'to be his followers too?"

Then they commenced to cussin' somethin' fierce, y'all. "Yer 'ees follower. We follow Moses. We know sure 'nuff God talked to Moses, but we don't know a dad burned thing 'bout this here feller."

"Well don't that just beat all!" the man answered. "Ye know he healed me don't ye? Well, God don't listen to no sinners, he listens to folks that praise 'eem and do what he tells 'em to. Never in all a history has someone been able to make a man that was blind all 'ees life to see. If'n this feller did'n come from God, He could'na done it."

. "Ye ain't nuthin' but a low down dirty sinner. And yer gonna sit there and lecture us!" and they kicked 'eem out a the church.

When Jesus heard 'bout it, he hunted the feller up and says, "Do ye trust the Son a Man?"

"Reckon who is he, sir. I sure would like to." the feller answered up.

"Ye saw 'eem" Jesus says, "matter a fact, he's talkin' to ye."

"Yes, Lord" the feller sad "sure 'nuff I believe!" and the feller had church right then and there.

Then Jesus told 'eem, "I done come to judge ever'body. I done come to make blind folks see and to tell folks that thinks they can see pretty good that they's really blind." The religious big shots was there and says, "So ye think we're blind do ye?"

"If'n y'all really could'n see then ye'd be alright in my book, but since ye say ye can see, then I reckon y'all are misbehavin'." Jesus answered. "Sure 'nuff, anybody that sneeks in the sheep pen, instead a goin' through the door, is up to no good. Cuz shepherds come in through the door. The door man's gonna open up the door fer 'eem and the sheep know 'eem by the way he talks and they come to 'eem. He knows ever' one of 'em's name and they follow 'eem out. Onced he's got all his sheep, he goes on ahead and they follow behind, cuz they know 'eem by 'ees voice. They won't come to a feller they don't know, cuz the don't know 'ees voice."

'Course they did'n understand what he was sayin', so he kindly told 'em what he meant. "Sure nuff, y'all. I'm the door" he says. "Ever'body else that come was aimin' to steal the sheep. But the real sheep did'n follow 'em. Yep, I'm the door. The folks that come through me's gonna git saved. They come on in and then they go on out again, but they always got some vittles. The ones that's up to no good is aimin' to tear the place up and kill my sheep. I'm just aimin' to give folks the good life."

"I'm the shepherd that really loves y'all. I love my sheep enough to die fer 'em. Somebody that's in it fer themselves is gonna up and run when the wolves come. He's gonna run off cuz they ain't really his sheep anyway so what does he care. So here comes the wolf, just a rippin' ever'thing up and runnin' the sheep off. The feller that's in it fer 'eemself is gonna up and run off, cuz he don't give a hill a beans 'bout them there sheep."

"I'm the shepherd that really loves y'all. I know who my little sheep is, and they know who I am. Just like me and my Daddy know one 'nuther. I'd die fer my little ole sheep. I have me some other sheep too, and they don't live 'round here. I'm gonna go git them too, and they's gonna hear me and come when I call, and we's all gonna live together and I'm gonna take care of 'em."

"The Daddy loves me cuz I'm willin' to die fer folks and then to make a come back. Nobody can kill me, less'n I let 'em. I'm able to give up my life when I won't to and then to make a comeback when I won't to. This here's what my Daddy told me to do."

When he says all that, the folks did'n really know what to make
of 'eem. Some folks says, "That fellers either got a booger in 'eem or
'ees a nutcase. What are y'all even listenin' to this feller fer?" Other
folks says, "Ye know, he don't sound like a man that's got a booger in
'eem. Can boogers make blind folks see?"

"My Daddy Can Whip Anybody"

It was winter time now, and Jesus was visitin' in Jerusalem fer
Hannukah. He was strollin' through the Temple over yonder by
Solomon's Porch. The Jewish religious big shots kindly come and
ganged up on 'eem and says, "Reckon how long are ye gonna beat
around the bush? If'n yer the King, just come right out and say it!"

Jesus answered up, "I done already told y'all, and ye don't
believe me. The proof is what I'm doin' fer my Daddy. But y'all don't
believe me cuz y'all ain't my sheep. My sheep knows my voice, and I
know them too, and they go where I lead. I give 'em the good life, and
they ain't never gonna die. Nobody is gonna up an grab 'em outta my
hand neither, cuz my Daddy give 'em to me and he can whip anybody.
By they way y'all, me and my Daddy is one and the same."

One more time, they grabbed some rocks to chuck 'em at 'eem and kill 'eem.

Jesus says, "Cuz my Daddy told me to, I done a whole bunch a good stuff fer the folks. Reckon which one a them things y'all aim to kill me fer?"

They huffed, "We ain't aimin' to kill ye fer doin' good stuff, but cuz ye done gone and says yer God, when ye ain't nuthin' but a man!"

Jesus answered up, "Y'alls own Bible says that God told certain folk 'I say y'all are gods'! And y'all know that the good book cain't be wrong. So if'n the good Lord called those folks gods, then why do y'all hollar heresy when the Holy feller brung here by the Daddy says, "I'm the Son a God". Y'all ort not to believe me unless I'm doin' the Daddy's work. But if'n I'm doin' the Daddy's work then even if y'all don't believe me, at least y'ort to believe the work I done. Then y'all will finally git it, that I'm in the Daddy and the Daddy is in me."

And again, they tried to bust 'eem, but he run off. He went on back over yonder past the Jordan River where it all started with John a dunkin' folks and such. A whole bunch a folks come over to 'eem and says "Ole John never did no mir'cles, but ever'thang he ever said 'bout this feller's done come true." And a whole mess a folks trusted 'eem.

Jesus Raises 'Ees Ole Buddy Lazarus

They was a feller by the name a Lazarus who was ailin' somethin' fierce. He lived over yonder in Bethany with Mary and Martha, 'ees sisters. This here's the same Mary that up and rinched 'ees feet off with perfume and let down her hair to sop it up. Ole Lazarus, her brother, was ailin'. So them two sisters sent Jesus this here message, "Lord, yer good buddy is ailin'."

When the message got to Jesus he says, "This here bug that Lazarus got, ain't a gonna have no sad endin' like death or nuthin'. God's fixin' to shine. Yep, the Son a God is fixin' to be in the spotlight on account a this." Jesus really was very fond a Mary and Martha and Ole Lazarus, but fer some reason he stayed right there fer two more days and did'n seem in no big hurry to get to 'em. Then he just up and says, "Let's go back to Judea, y'all."

But the disciples kindly thew a fit, "Rabbi, the other day they was fixin' to kill ye and now ye wanna go back?"

Jesus answered up, "They's a whole lot a daylight ever'day and when it's light outside folks is safe cuz they got the sun to light the way. But when night time comes that's when folks had better watch there step." The he says. "Lazarus has done fell asleep, y'all. I gotta go wake 'eem up."

The disciples hollared out, "But Lord, if'n he's asleep, he's gonna get better by and by!" They reckoned Jesus was sayin' Lazarus was restin', but what he meant was Lazarus had done passed away.

Then he did'n mince no words, "Lazarus is dead. And on account a y'all I'm glad I wud'n there cuz this here'll give ye one more chance to believe. C'mon, let's go see Lazarus."

Then Thomas (folks just called 'eem the Twin) says to the rest of the 'em "Ah ight, we're with ye. Come on y'all, let's go die with Jesus."

When Jesus got to Bethany they told 'eem Lazarus had done been buried four days. Bethany wud'n too fur down the road from Jerusalem so's a whole bunch a Jewish folks had done come out to hug Mary and Martha's neck and say goodbye to ole Lazarus.
When Martha heard that Jesus was a comin' she run out to see 'eem, but Mary stayed home. Martha says to Jesus, "Lord, if ye were here,

my brother would still be with us. But there' still hope even now. I know God'll answer yer prayers. "

Jesus says to her, "Yer brother's gonna git up."

"I know it, Lord. By and by on resurrection day he will, with the rest of us."

Jesus says to her, "Hun, I am the resurrection and I am the life. Folks who trust in me, even if they die, they's gonna git back up. They have the gift of livin' ferever and they don't have to ever fret over dyin'. Martha hun, do ye believe that?"

"Yeah, Lord" Martha says, "I shore do believe. I always believed ye was the King, the Son a God, fetched into this here world by God, eemself." Then she went on back to Mary. She took Mary over where they could be alone and says "Mary, the Rabbi has done come and he's lookin' fer ye." So Mary run off to find 'eem.

Now, Jesus had kindly stayed on the outskirts a town, where him and Martha had talked. When the folks saw Mary run off, they thought she was a goin' over to see Lazarus, so they come after her. When Mary got to Jesus she thowed herself down on 'ees feet and says, "Lord, My brother would'n a died if'n ye'd a been here!" When Jesus saw Mary and the rest a the folks a wailin' and a cryin' and a carryin' on, he plumb got upset.

"Where'd y'all put 'eem?" He asked 'em.

"Come, we'll show ye." They says.

Then Jesus commenced to ballin'.

The folks says, "Don't y'all see how much he loved ole Lazarus." But some folks says, "If'n he could make a blind feller see, don't ye think he might a been able to do somethin' fer ole Lazarus."

Jesus was really upset by the time they got to the grave. It was one a them there cave graves and with a big ole rock rolled in front a the door.

"Git rid a that rock" Jesus says.

Martha says, "Now, wait a minute Lord. He's been in there four days deader'n a hammer, and that smell's liable to light all of us up."

"Did'n I tell ye, y'all was fixin'to see God do some shinin' if'n y'all would believe?" So they rolled that big ole rock away. Then Jesus commenced to lookin' up into the sky and says, "Daddy, thankee kindly fer listenin' to me. Ye always got yer ears on, but I'm sayin' all this so these good folks here will believe that ye brung me."

Then Jesus just up and hollared, "Lazarus, come up outta there!" And sure 'nuff Lazarus come on out and still had his funeral garb on, lookin' kindly like a mummy so Jesus says, "Y'all take that stuff off of 'eem and turn 'eem loose!"

"Y'all Are All Just Dumber'na Bag a Hammers…
The Feller's Got to Die"

Many a the folks that was there fer Mary seen it and believed in Jesus. But, would'n ye know it, some of 'em run off and tattled on 'eem to the religious big shots so they called a meetin' and says, "What in the world are we gonna do here? This feller no doubt does a whole bunch a mir'cles. If'n we don't do somethin' this is fixin'to plumb git outta hand and then the Roman army's gonna come and kick our tails real good and wreck the whole country and the Temple too!"

Then ole Caiaphas, the head religious feller says, "Y'all are all just dumber'na bag a hammers. It's plain what we gotta do. The fellers got to die fer the good a the people." Now, actually Caiaphas bein' the head religious feller and all was kindly inspired by God to say that, it was actually a perdiction that Jesus was fixin'to die not only fer the Jews, but fer the whole world to bring folks together under 'ees rule as one nation. So from then on they was a plottin' to kill 'eem. So Jesus kindly went into hidin'. He run off into the country with 'ees disciples to Eprhaim and stayed fer a spell.

Now, it was round 'bout time fer the Passover and folks packed into Jerusalem in droves from the country and got there early so's they could commence to preparin' themselves with what they called a cleanin' ceremony. Ever'body was lookin' fer Jesus to show up and they says, "Y'all reckon he's gonna be here fer the Passover?" And the religious big shots had done said if anybody sees 'eem they gotta turn 'eem in to the cops.

Mary Warshes Jesus' Feet With High Falutin' Perfume

Six days before the Passover Jesus come to Bethany to Lazarus' house, the feller he brought back to life. They made a dinner fer 'eem, and Martha was servin' ever'body and Lazarus was right there at the table with 'em. Then Mary took some real high-falutin' rich folk perfume and warshed Jesus' feet with it and dried 'em off with her hair and the whole house smelled real good. But ole Judas, the turncoat, says, "That there perfume cost a bundle, we could a sold that and give the money to the poor." He really did'n give a hill a beans 'bout poor folks, he was in charge a the funds, and he used to dip into 'em and give it the five finger discount whenever he took a notion to.

Jesus answered up, "Get off her case, feller. Y'alls always gonna have the poor, but ye ain't always gonna have me."

When all the folks heard that Jesus was back in town they showed up in droves to see 'eem and to see ole Lazarus who'd come back from the dead. And the religious big shots decided they might ort to kill him too, cuz he was the reason all the folks was leavin' them and goin' to Jesus.

Long live the King a Israel!

The next day it spread like wildfire that Jesus was back in town and headed fer Jerusalem. A big ole crowd a folks took palm leaves and went down the road to meet 'eem. They commenced to shoutin' "Praise the Lord! Blessed is the feller that comes speakin' fer God. Long live the King a Israel!" Jesus found 'eem a little ole donkey and kept that prophecy 'bout "Don't fret, folks from Israel. Here comes yer king, just a ridin' a little ole donkey."

The disciples wud'n thinkin' 'bout prophecy much at the time though, but after he went on home to glory they 'membered that they

60

had seen what the good book predicted 'sure nuff with their very own eyes!

The folks that had seen ole Lazarus come back to life was just a jabberin'. That's why so many folks come out to meet 'eem, cuz they heard 'bout what he'd done. Then the religious big shots says, "Well, stick a fork in us cuz we's done. Would ye just look at that. The whole world is out there!"

Some Greek folks come to see Phillip who come from Bethsaida over yonder in Galilee. They says, "Feller, we sure would like to meet ole Jesus." Phillip told Andrew and they both run and asked Jesus 'bout it.

Jesus answered up, "I reckon it's 'bout time fer the Son a Man to commence to shinin'. Sure 'nuff, y'all, less'n a kernel a wheat falls and dies it's just gonna keep on bein' one little seed. But if'n it dies it's gonna be a whole harvest a brand new shiny folks. But, folks who keep holdin' on to life in this ole world are gonna lose it. Folks who turn loose are gonna keep it ferever. All y'all that wanna be my followers got to come after me, cuz my folks got to be where I am. If'n y'all come after me, the Daddy is gonna honor ye. Now, I'm kindly upset right now, y'all. What am I s'posed to do? Am I s'posed to pray,

61

Lord, save me from what's 'bout to happen? I cain't very well do that when it's the reason I come in the first place. So I'll just say, Daddy commence to shinin'."

Then there come a voice from up yonder in heaven sayin' "I already been shinin'. And, I'm fixin' to shine some more." When all the folks heard it, some of 'em says it was thunder and some says it was an angel talkin' to 'eem.

Then Jesus told 'em, "That there voice y'all just heard wud'n fer me, it was fer y'all. Judgment time has come, and I'm fixin' to kick the devils tail right outta here. And when I done been toted up on that cross, I'm fixin' to reel ever'body in." He says this to tell folks how he was fixin' to die.

"Why ye talkin' bout dyin'" says the folks. "We thought the good book says the King was gonna live ferever. What's all this talk 'bout the Son a Man dyin'? Reckon who are ye talkin' 'bout when ye say Son a Man?"

Jesus answered up, "I'm gonna be here shinin' just a little bit longer y'all. Waller in the light while ye can, so's ye won't trip and fall when it get's dark. Folks that walk in the dark is bound to fall down.

Trust in this here light while ye got it, then y'all will become my shiny kids." Once he done said all that, he run off and hid out fer a little bit.

But in spite a ever'thang that he'd done- all the mir'cles and wunnerful stuff, most folks still did'n put their trust in 'eem. Back yonder in the Isaiah that's exactly what he says was gonna happen: "Lord, reckon who is even gonna believe this here message? And who ye gonna show yer strong savin' power to?"

So the folks could'n believe cuz ole Isaiah had also said back yonder, "The Lord made 'em blind, and he made their hearts hard. So they cain't see nuthin' ner understand it all, less'n they come to their senses and let me heal 'em."

Ole Isaiah was talkin' 'bout Jesus and kindly predictin' the future when he says all that cuz he seen a vision a The King's shinin'. Many folks put their trust in 'eem and even some a them ole religious big shots. But they did'n talk 'bout it much cuz they was skeert they'd get put out a the church. They was kindly too worried 'bout what folks thought of 'em, and not enough 'bout what God thought of 'em.

Jesus commenced to hollarin', "If'n y'all trust in me, yer trustin' in God who fetched me. Cuz when ye look at me, ye're lookin' at the feller that sent me. I come to do some shinin' in this hear ole dark world, so y'all won't have to keep on stumblin' 'round in the dark. And if'n a feller hears what I got to say and don't believe it, I ain't come to judge 'eem. That ain't what I come fer. I come to save folks. The feller that don't trust what I got to say, well, it's them there words themselves that'll judge 'eem at the end a time. Cuz I had'n been talkin' my own words. These are the words a my Daddy that fetched me. He told me ever'thang that I was s'posed to say and how I was s'posed to say it. And I know that what he tells folks to do leads to the good life. So, y'all see, ever'thang I done told y'all is exactly what my Daddy told me to say."

Jesus Warshes They's Feet

Now, the Passover was right around the corner. Jesus reckoned it was 'bout time fer 'eem to be headin' on outta here and back to 'ees Daddy. He'd done loved on the folks that belonged to 'eem over here in this ole world and now it was time to show 'em just how much he loved 'em. It was 'bout time fer supper, and ole Slew Foot had done whispered in Judas ear to go ahead and do 'ees dirty work. Jesus knowed that the good Lord had done put 'eem in charge a ever'thang and that he had come from God and it was almost time to be moseyin' back home. So he kindly rose up and run 'eem some water in a big ole bowl and took 'ees robe off and tied a towel round 'ees midlands. Then he commenced to warshin' the disciples feet and soppin' up the water with that there towel. When he come to ole Simon Rocky, he says, "Lord, y'ort not be warshin' my feet!"

And Jesus says to 'eem, "I know ye don't really understand this right now, but some day yer gonna."

And Rocky answered up, "Huh, uh! Ye ain't fixin' to warsh my feet!"

Jesus says, "Less'n I warsh these here feet, ye ain't none a mine."

Then Rocky up and hollared, "Aw, just g'on and warsh all a me while yer at it, then!"

Jesus answered 'eem, "Now, folks that's had a bath don't need warshin' 'cept fer they's feet, and then they'll be all clean. And sure 'nuff y'all are clean, 'cept fer one a ye." Cuz Jesus already knowed who was up to no good, that's what he was talkin' 'bout when he says, "cept fer one a ye."

After he got through warshin' feet, he put on 'ees robe and says, "Did y'all git anything out a that there lesson? Y'all call me "Rabbi"

65

and "Lord" and that's all well and good, cuz I'm the boss. But look here y'all, since I served y'all, y'ort to serve one 'nuther. I gave y'all a little lesson there. Now, what I done fer y'all, do that fer one 'nuther, ah ight?"

"Boy, ain't it the truth y'all, that a worker ain't better than 'ees boss. And the feller that brung the message, cain't be better than the one that sent 'eem. Now, that I done taught y'all how it's done, serve one 'nuther like that and y'all be happy."

"I ain't really sayin' this stuff to all a y'all. I chose each and ever'one a y'all, so I know ye, 'sure nuff. The good book says, "The feller that has supper with me has done kicked me in the face", and I reckon that 'uns fixin' to come true. The reason I'm tellin' y'all 'fore it happens is cuz when it does I won't ye to believe that I'm the King. Sure 'nuff anybody that takes me in, takes in the feller that fetched me, and anybody that takes in the ones I'm fixin' to send out, takes me in."

After he'd done said that he kindly broke down sayin', "Sure 'nuff, one a y'all is fixin'to turn on me."

The disciples commenced to lookin' round at one 'nuther, wonderin' which one it was. This here disciple that Jesus shore did love was sittin' next to 'eem at the supper table. Ole Rocky kindly motioned fer 'eem to ask who would be such a low down turncoat. So, he bent over and says, "Lord, who's fixin' to do it."

Jesus answered "I'm fixin' to sop this here biscuit in gravy and the one I pass it down to is the one that's fixin' to do the dirty deed." And he sopped it in gravy and passed it right down to ole Judas, Simon Iscariot's boy. Judas wolfed it down with the gusto of a hound dawg and then Ole Slewfoot got into 'eem. Then Jesus just up and says, "Don't waste no time, let's go ahead and git it over with." But the other fellers did'n really know what he was talkin' 'bout. They reckoned since Judas kept the money bag and all, that Jesus wanted 'eem to go pay fer the food or give some money to poor folks. So ole Judas jumped up and run off into the dark.

"I Am How Y'all Git to Heaven. I Am The Only Way to Live."

After ole Judas run off, Jesus says, "I reckon it's time fer me to commence to shinin' and God's gonna shine too cuz a all that's fixin' to happen to me. And God's gonna cause me to shine real soon, y'all."

"My sweet young 'uns, I got to be moseyin' on down the road. Y'all are gonna come a lookin' fer me, but y'all ain't gonna find me- just like I told them religious fellers. Y'all cain't go with me neither.

On account a I ain't gonna be here to love on ye, I won't y'all to love on one 'nuther. That's there's the new commandment I'm a givin' y'all. Love one 'nuther. Y'all seen how I always loved on ye. Now, I won't y'all to love on one 'nuther the same way. That there down home love fer one 'nuther is a gonna be y'alls callin' card to prove y'all are really my folks."

Ole Simon Rocky says, "Lord, where ye goin"?

And Jesus told 'eem, "Ye cain't come with me now, but y'all can come on later."

"I don't see why I cain't come on with ye now." Rocky says. "I'd take a bullet fer ye, Lord."

"Ye'd take a bullet fer me would ye? 'Fore this here night is over, three times yer gonna deny that ye even know me."

"Don't fret 'bout nuthin', though, y'all. Y'all trust God, now trust me too. I'm a tellin' it to ye straight y'all, my Daddy's got a big ole mansion and they's a whole bunch a rooms, and I'm gonna run on ahead and git it ready fer y'all. When I git all done, I'm a gonna come back and git y'all, so's we won't never be apart no more. Now y'all know where I'm a goin' and ye know how to git there."

And then ole Thomas chimed in, "Lord, we don't know nary a thang 'bout where yer goin' so how in the world are we gonna know how to git there?"

"I am how y'all git to heaven. I am the only way to live. Nobody gits to the Daddy 'cept by me. If y'all would a knowed me, ye'd a knowed my Daddy, but I reckon y'all will know 'eem from here on out, cuz ye done seen 'eem.

And ole Phillip says, "Lord, I reckon we'd like to meet the Daddy. That'll be enough proof fer us."

And Jesus answered up, "Phillip, ye mean to tell me after all this time ye don't even see me fer who I really am? If'n ye seen me, ye seen the Daddy. So, why in the world would ye ask to meet 'eem? Don't y'all believe that my Daddy is in me and I'm in my Daddy. I ain't been tellin' stuff I made up myownself, my Daddy is a doin' all this stuff from inside me. So, y'all just believe that I'm in my Daddy and my Daddy is in me. If'n ye cain't do nuthin' else believe in the mir'cles y'all seen me do."

"I Ain't A Gonna Leave Y'all Alone Without Nobody to Care Fer Ye"

"No doubt 'bout it y'all, anybody who believes in me is fixin' to do some of the same stuff I dun done and even better stuff cuz I'm a goin' home to my Daddy and y'all can ask fer anything on account a me and I'll just up and do it, cuz I aim to make my Daddy shine. So sure 'nuff, anything y'all ask me to do, I'm gonna just up and do it."

"If'n ye love me, just do what I tell ye to. And, I'm a gonna go to my Daddy and ask 'eem to send y'all a therapist to live on the inside and never leave. He's the Holy Spirit, come to teach y'all the truth. The world cain't get in on this cuz they ain't lookin' fer 'eem and ain't gonna know 'eem when He comes. But y'all do, cuz He's right here with ye now, and later he's gonna be inside ye. Naw, I ain't gonna leave y'all alone without nobody to care fer ye, I'm a gonna come be inside ye."

"Here in a bit, I'm fixin' to make myself scarce, but y'all are gonna know where I am. Fer I'm just gonna up and come back to life, and y'all are gonna be full a life too. When I come back to life, it's gonna dawn on ye that I'm in the Daddy and y'all are in me and I'm in y'all. Folks that do what I tell 'em to is the ones that love me. And because a that there love fer me, my Daddy is gonna love 'em and I'm a gonna love 'em too. And I'm a gonna come visit with those folks.

Ole Judas (not Judas Iscariot, but the other feller by the name a Judas) up and says, "Lord, reckon why yer gonna just come visit with us and not ever'body."

Jesus anwered up, "Folks that love me' is a gonna do what I tell 'em to. My Daddy's gonna love 'em and we's gonna move in and stay with 'em. Folks that don't love me, ain't gonna do what I tell 'em to. And 'member y'all I ain't just makin' all this up on the fly. My Daddy told me to say all this. Whilst I'm still with y'all, I'm tellin' all this stuff. But Daddy's gonna send the therapist on account a me, and He's gonna teach y'all 'bout ever'thang, and remind y'all 'bout all this I done said too."

I'm leavin' y'all with peace, y'all can have it free a charge. Not like ye git stuff in this here ole world. So, don't y'all worry 'bout a thing and don't be skeert neither. Y'all done heard me say, "I got to be moseyin' on" but I'm a gonna come on back to y'all. If y'all really love me, y'all are gonna be cheerin' fer me cuz I git to go back to my Daddy, who's the best. I'm tellin' y'all stuff 'fore it happens, so's when it does happen, y'all will believe.

I really ain't got much more time left, y'all. Cuz ole Slewfoot is a comin' fer me. I could whip 'eem if'n I took a notion to, but I gotta do what my Daddy tells me to, so's everybody'll know that I love my Daddy. Now, come on. Let's git outta here.

"True Believers Is Gonna Bring a Mess a Fruit."

"Now, I'm the tree, y'all, and my Daddy's the farmer. He chops off ever' branch that ain't got no fruit on it, and he trims the ones that does got fruit so they'll grow even more fruit. Y'all done been trimmed cuz a ever'thang I done told ye. Now, y'all stay ri-cheer in me and I'll stay in you. Cuz a branch cain't grow no fruit if'n it is cut off from the tree, and y'all cain't grow no fruit less'n ye stay ri-cheer in me."

"Sure 'nuff, I'm the tree, and y'all are the branches. Folks who stay in me, and I stay in them's gonna grow a whole mess a fruit. Cuz y'all cain't do nuthin' without me. Folks that up and run off is like a old dead branch that fell off the tree. They's just garbage to be disposed of. But if y'all stay ri-cheer in me and my words stay in you, y'all can just up and ask fer anything and I'll do it. True believers is gonna bring a mess a fruit. And this here is gonna make the Daddy shine."

"Now, I have loved y'all somethin' fierce, just like my Daddy loves me. Y'all stay in my love. When ye do what I tell ye to, y'all will stay in my love, just like when I do what my Daddy says I stay in His love. I'm a tellin' y'all this so's y'all can be brimmin' with my joy. Sure 'nuff y'alls joy's gonna spill out all over the place. Now, here's what I won't y'all to do. Love one 'nuther somethin' fierce, just like I have loved y'all. Ain't no love better than to give up yer life fer yer buddies. Y'all are my buddies, if'n y'all do what I tell ye to. I ain't even gonna call y'all my hired help no more, cuz the boss don't tell 'ees hired help all 'ees business. Y'all are my pals, cuz I done told y'all ever'thang my Daddy told me. Y'all did'n just up and decide to choose me, cuz I had done already chose y'all. I chose y'all to grow some fruit that ain't gonna never rurn, so's the Daddy'll give ye whatever ye ask fer on account a me. This here's what I'm a tellin' y'all to do. Love one 'nuther."

"Now, if'n the world commences to hatin' on y'all, remember they was hatin' on me first. The world would love y'all if'n y'all was like ever'body else, but I done called y'all to be rebels, so they's gonna

73

hate on ye. Don't y'all remember what I told ye 'bout 'the hired help ain't greater than the boss.' Well since they come after me with guns a blazin', they's a gonna come after y'all too. And if'n they'd listened to me, they'll listen to y'all too. Folks in the world is gonna be hatin' on y'all, just cuz yer mine, and cuz they don't know the feller that fetched me. It might not be so bad if'n I had'n come and visited with 'em, but since I did, they ain't got no excuse fer all their misbehavin'."

"Folks that hate on me, hate on my Daddy too. If'n I had'n done all these mir'cles amongst 'em they would'n be seen as doin' wrong, but even after all they seen, they still hated on me and my Daddy. But this here is the good book comin' true, cuz it says, "they just up and hated me fer nuthin'.""

"But I'm a gonna send y'all the therapist- the Spirit a truth. The Daddy's gonna fetch 'eem and he'll tell y'all all 'bout me. And Y'all got to tell folks 'bout me too, 'cause y'all been here from the very start."

"I told y'all all a this stuff so's ye won't git frustrated and just up and quit. Cuz they's gonna put y'all out a the church, and 'fore too long folks is gonna think they's doin' God's work if'n they just up and kill ye. That's cuz they's ignernt a me and my Daddy. Sure 'nuff,

I'm a tellin' y'all this so's when it happens y'all are gonna 'member I told ye so. I would a already told ye, but I was gonna be here for y'all a little bit longer."

"But now I got to be moseyin' on home to the feller that fetched me, and y'all ain't even asked me where I'm a goin'. But, y'all look like ye just lost yer best friend. But it ain't a bad thing, y'all. If'n I don't go, the therapist ain't a gonna come. But if I run on home, I'll send 'eem yer way. When he gits here he's gonna commence to convincin' folks that they's been misbehavin' cuz a sin and the good Lord's righteousness, and the judgment that's fixin to come up on this here world. Folks sin is that they don't trust in me. Righteousness is y'alls fer the askin' cuz I'm fixin'to head on home to the Daddy and make myself scarce. Judgment's gonna come cuz Ole Slew Foot has done been dealt with."

"Buck Up Y'all. I Done Whipped the World!"

"Aw, they's so much more I wanna tell y'all, but ye ain't ready to hear it. When the Spirit a truth comes a callin', he'll tell ye lots more. He ain't a gonna give y'all 'ees own ideers, but He's a gonna tell y'all what he's done heard. He'll even tell y'all 'bout stuff that ain't happened yet. He's a gonna make me shine by showin' y'all what I tell 'eem to. All my Daddy's stuff is mine too, so that's why I says the Spirit's gonna tell y'all what he got from me. After while, I'm fixin' to make myself scarce and then a little bit later I'm a gonna come on back."

The disciples commenced to askin' one 'nuther, "Reckon what in the world He is talkin' 'bout then he says 'I'm fixin' to make myself scarce, and I'll be back.' And what 'bout, 'I'm a goin' to my Daddy.' And reckon what he means by 'a little bit.' We's just plumb bumfuzzled."

Jesus seen they was kindly strugglin' with ever'thang so he says, "Are y'all wonderin' what I was talkin' 'bout when I says in a little bit I'm fixin' to make myself scarce, and then a little bit later I'm a gonna come back? Sure 'nuff y'all are gonna be ballin' and grievin' 'bout what's fixin' to happen to me, even while ever'body else is celebratin'. Y'all are gonna be real sad, but then y'all will just up and be happy when I come back. Kindly like a lady givin' birth. It sure does hurt, but when it's over she don't even pay it no mind, cuz she's done brung a new life into this here world."

"Y'all are sad now, but when I come on back yer gonna want to thow a party and nobody'll be able to take that good feelin' away from ye. Round about then, y'all won't need to ask me fer nuthin'. Sure 'nuff, y'all can go right to yer Daddy and ask and he'll give y'all whatever yer askin' fer, on account a me. Y'all ain't done it this way up 'til now. Go 'head on and ask on account a me and ye'll git it, and a whole mess a joy to boot."

"Now, I kindly been teachin' y'all by tellin' stories, but times a comin' when I'm a gonna tell it to ye straight 'bout my Daddy. That's when y'all are gonna ask on account a me. I ain't sayin' it's gonna be me doin' the askin'. The Daddy loves y'all somethin' fierce cuz y'all loved me and believe that I come from God. Sure 'nuff y'all, I come from the Daddy into this Ole World and I'm fixin' to mosey on back home to my Daddy."

Then 'ees disciples says, "Finally yer tellin' it straight and not usin' no stories. Now, I reckon we git it. Ye don't need nobody to tell ye nuthin' cuz ye already know ever'thang. On account a that, we reckon ye did come from God."

Jesus answered up "Well, it's 'bout time, y'all got it! But it's fixin' to git ugly. Y'all are gonna up and leave me and run off on yer own. But it'll be ah ight cuz I won't really be alone. My Daddy'll be with me. I told y'all all this stuff so's y'all could be at peace. In this ole world y'all are gonna have some real hard times. But buck up y'all. I done whipped the world!"

King Jesus Prays fer 'em One Last Time

When Jesus got done talkin' he kindly looked up to the sky and says, "Daddy, I reckon it's 'bout time. Make yer boy shine so's he can make ye shine. Fer ye done made 'eem King over all the earth so's he can give the good life to all the folks that ye give to 'eem. And this here's the way to live ferever- to know ye, the only real God, and King Jesus the one ye fetched to planet earth. I made ye shine here, cuz I done ever'thang that ye told me to. And now, Daddy, bring me on home to that shiny place where we always lived, even before this here world got started."

"I done told these fellers 'bout ye. They come right up outta this here world to be mine, cuz ye give 'em to me and they done what ye told 'em to. They knowed I ain't got nuthin' that ye did'n give to me, and I done told 'em ever'thang ye told me to and they just up and believed all of it- how ye fetched me down here and how I come from ye and all."

"I ain't fixin' to pray fer the world, I'm fixin' to pray fer them that ye give me, cuz they's yers. What's yers is mine and what's mine is yers so these here fellers is yers too. Ye give 'em to me, and they's my pride and joy!"

"Now, I got to be moseyin' on home to ye, and leave 'em behind. Holy Daddy, hold 'em close and look after 'em, so's they'll be just as close as we are. While I was ri-cheer with 'em, I took good care of 'em. I kept watch over 'em like a ole hound dawg and did'n lose nary a one, 'cept the one that was bound and determined to work 'ees way to hell, just like the good book said he would."

"I'm fixin' to come on home now. I done told 'em all kind a stuff so's they would shine with my joy. I give 'em yer word. The world hates on 'em cuz they's rebels, just like me. I ain't askin' ye to take 'em outta here, but I'm askin' ye to keep 'em safe from ole Slew Foot whilst they's here. They's rebels far as this ole world is concerned, just like me. Kindly clean 'em up fer me by teachin' 'em yer words a truth. Ye sent me into this ole world and I'm sendin' these fellers. I'm fixin' to give up ever'thang fer ye, so's they can be completely yers."

"I ain't just prayin' fer these fellers neither but fer ever' believer from here on out that's gonna up and believe cuz a the story they's gonna tell. My prayer is that all of 'em would stick together, just like you and me stuck together, Daddy. I pray they stick with us- you in me, me in you, and them in us- so's the whole world'll know ye fetched me."

"I made 'em shiny like ye made me shiny, so's they would stick together- me in them and you in me, just one big ole happy fam'ly- that way the world'll know ye fetched me and love them just the same as ye love me. Daddy, I won't these fellers to be with me in heaven so's they can see me shine. Ye been makin' me shine cuz a yer love since way back yonder 'fore the world even got started!"

"Oh, righteous Daddy, the world don't even know ye, but I do, and these here disciples know ye fetched me. I done showed ye to 'em and I aim to keep on showin' 'em. I'm a gonna do it so's yer love fer me will git into 'em. And I reckon I'll just git into 'em myownself."

Judas, The Turncoat, Turns King Jesus In

After he done said all that, Jesus come across the Kidron valley with 'ees disciples and went off into a holler a olive trees. Ole Judas, the turncoat, knowed 'bout this here place cuz Jesus used to go there all the time with 'ees disciples. All the high-falutin' religious folk had give 'eem a mess a Roman soldiers and some a the Temple Cops to come with 'eem. Now they come after 'eem in the holler all bowed up with guns drawed and torches and what not.

Jesus knowed all that was 'bout to happen and come out to meet 'em bold as anything and asked 'em, "Who y'all lookin' fer?"

"Jesus a Nazareth", they answered.

"Yer lookin' at 'eem", Jesus says, "God in the flesh." (Judas, the turncoat, was with 'em too when Jesus said that.) And when he says, "God in the flesh" it knocked 'all of 'em right back on their hind ends.

One more time he says, "Who y'all lookin' fer?"

And they says again, "Jesus a Nazareth,"

"I done told y'all it was me", Jesus answered. "If'n y'all are lookin' fer me, let these other fellers go." He done that to make 'ees own story come true that, "I ain't lost a single one ye give to me."

Then ole Simon Rocky heaved out 'ees sword and lopped off the right ear a Malchus, a feller that worked fer the High Priest. But Jesus told Rocky, "Put up yer sword, now. I got to do what the Daddy give me to do."

So the soldiers and the cops arrested Jesus and put 'eem in hand cuffs. The first place they took 'eem was to Annas, father-in-law a Caiaphas, the High Priest fer that year. Caiaphas was the feller that had told the other religious big shots "better that one feller die fer ever'body."

Ole Rocky Denies Jesus

Rocky and another one a the disciples kindly follered behind a ways. That other feller knowed the high priest, so they let 'eem come into the courtyerd with Jesus, whilst Rocky stayed behind. Then that other feller says somethin' or 'nuther to the lady watchin' the gate and she let Rocky in. The lady asked ole Rocky, "Ain't ye one them disciples a Jesus?"

"Naw" he says, "I ain't neither."

Some a the guards and hired help was standin' round by a fire they had made cuz if was kindly chilly outside. Ole Rocky just slipped right in with 'em and warmed 'ees hands by the fire.

In the house, the high priest commenced to grillin' Jesus 'bout 'ees followers and teachin's and what not. Jesus answered 'eem, " It ain't no secret what I teach, I done preached in the churches and the Temple and ever'where else. I ain't got nuthin' to hide. Why'd y'all haul me in to ask such a thang? Ye could a asked anybody that heard me preach. Ever'body knows what I been teachin'. One a the Temple Cops standin' there punched 'eem in the nose. "That ain't no kinda way to be talkin' to the high priest!" he hollared.

"What'd I say that was so wrong? Y'all punch folks around here fer tellin' the truth?" Jesus said.

Then Annas had 'eem tied up and sent 'eem off to Caiaphas, the high priest.

Meanwhile, as Rocky was keepin' warm by the fire, they asked 'eem, "Hey, ain't ye one of 'ees discples?"

"I ain't neither", he answered up.

But one a the hired help spoke up who was kin to the feller who's ear Rocky had cut off, "I knowed I seen ye somewhere before. Wud'n ye out yonder in the holler with Jesus?" But ole Rocky denied it one more time and no sooner had he got the words out a his mouth than a rooster crowed.

"What in Tarnation is Truth?"

By the time Caiaphas got through with 'eem it was early mornin'. Then they took 'eem to the Roman governor's mansion. The folks that was accusin' 'eem did'n even go in, cuz it was agin' their religion to be amongst heatherns and they wanted to be able to go to the Passover shindig. So ole Pilate, the governor, come out to 'em asked, "What y'all got against this feller?"

"Well, it's obvious he's a criminal ain't it or we would'n a drug 'eem in here in the first place!" they hollared.

"Then why don't ye drag 'eem off and try 'eem in yer own court", says Pilate.

"We'd druther ye did it, cuz only the Romans can impose the death penalty" the Jewish religious folk replied. This here made Jesus' 'foretellin' come true 'but how he was fixin' to die.

Then ole Pilate went back in the house and had 'em bring Jesus in there.

"Well, are ye the Jewish King or not?" he asked 'eem.

Jesus answered, "Where'd ye get that ideer? Did ye come up with that yerownself or did somebody tell ye?"

"Am I Jewish?" he says. "Yer very own folks and their religious leaders brung ye in here. Tell me why they done it. What did ye do?"

Jesus answered eem, "My kingdom ain't from 'round here. If'n it was ye can be sure my folks would a fought fer me when I was drug in by the Jewish religious big shots. But my kingdom ain't from 'round here."

"So, y'are a King are ye?" Pilate says.

"Ye done said a mouthful, cuz I was born fer that very thing. And I come to tell it to folks straight, no stretchers. Ever'body that won'ts the truth, won'ts to hear what I got to say."

"What in tarnation is truth?" says ole Pilate. Then he come outside and told the Jews, "He ain't guilty a nuthin', but y'all have this here tradition to turn somebody loose ever' year at the Passover. Y'all won't me to turn loose the King a the Jews?"

But they hollared back at 'eem, "No way! Turn loose a ole Barabbas!" (Barabbas was in jail fer tryin' to overthrow the government). Then Pilate told 'em to take Jesus away and whip 'eem. The soldiers kindly made a crown out a some stickers and put it on 'ees head, and they put a purple robe on 'eem.

"All Hail, the King a the Jews!", they jabbed, as they punched 'eem in the nose.

Pilate come outside again and says to the folks, "I'm fixin' to bring 'eem back out, on account a I don't see where he done anything wrong." Then Jesus come out with the crown a stickers and the purple robe on. Pilate says, "Just look at this feller".

When the religious big shots and Temple Cops seen 'eem, they hollared out, "Crucify 'eem! Crucify 'eem!"

"Y'all crucify 'eem yerownselves, dad gummit! I don't see where he done nuthin' wrong!" Pilate answered back.

The Jewish religious big shots says, "Cuz a our religious laws he ort to die, cuz he said he was the Son a God."

Well, when ole Pilate heard that, boy that really put a scare in 'eem. He took Jesus back in the house and says, "Where in the world did ye come from?" But Jesus did'n have nuthin' to say.

"Speak up feller! Don't ye know who yer talkin' to? I could release ye if I took a notion to or else crucify ye!" Pilate says.

"Ye ain't got nuthin' on me, mister, that ye did'n git from on high. So, I reckon the feller that turned me in is the one that sinned the worst" says Jesus.

86

Then Pilate tried to turn 'eem loose, but the Jews just kept on

hollarin' "If'n ye release this feller, ye sure ain't no friend a Ceasar.

Any feller that says he's a King is rebellin' against Ceasar."

When Pilate heard all that, he fetched Jesus out and sit down on

the judgement seat on what's called the Stone Pavement (called

Gabbatha in Hebrew). It was 'round 'bout six in the mornin' on the

day a gittin' ready fer the Passover. Pilate says to the folks, "Ri-cheers

yer King, y'all!"

"Git 'eem out a here!" they hollared. "Crucify 'eem!"

"Ye mean to tell me y'all won't me to crucify yer King?"

Pilated asked.

"We ain't got no King, 'cept fer Ceasar", the head religious

folks hollared back.

King Jesus Up and Hollars, "Paid In Full"!

Then ole Pilate give 'em Jesus so's they could crucify 'eem.

The soldiers took 'eem and led 'eem off. Jesus toted 'ees own cross

and went over yonder to Skull Hill (Golgotha, in Hebew) where they

run railroad spikes through 'ees hands and feet into the wood and stood

'eem upright to die. They was two other fellers with 'eem on either side and Jesus was betwixt 'em. Ole Pilate had 'em put a sign over 'ees head that read, "Jesus a Nazareth, King a the Jews". Where they crucified 'eem was just outside the city and they wrote it in Hebrew, Greek, and Latin so's ever'body could read it. The religious big shots kindly pitched a fit to Pilate, "Don't say he was King a the Jews. Say he claimed he was King a the Jews." But Pilate answered up, "I done wrote all I aim to write".

When the soldier had done crucified 'eem, they divied up 'ees clothes 'mongst the four of 'em. And they took 'ees robe, which was just one piece and says, "Y'all, let's not rip it up, let's thow dice to see who gits to keep it." This here made the good book come true where it says, "They divied up my clothes and thowed dice fer my robe." So that's how they done it.

Standin' not too fer off was Jesus' momma and her sister Mary (Ole Clopas' wife) and Mary Magdalene. When Jesus saw 'ees Momma standin' yonder beside the disciple he shore did love, he up and says, "Hun, this here's yer boy now." And he says to yonder disciple, "This here's yer momma, now." And from then on out, that there disciple took her in and made her feel right at home.

Jesus knowed all 'ees work was done, so to make the good book come true he says, "I'm kindly thirsty." A jar a vinegar wine was sittin' there so's they stuck it on the end of a hyssop plant and put it on 'ees lips. After he'd done tasted some, he just up and hollared out, "Paid in full!" and bowed 'ees head and turned loose a his spirit.

Cuz a the Passover and the Sabbath and all, the religious big shots reckoned they did'n won't no dead bodies hangin' 'round to dirty up the place so's they asked Pilate to order they's legs broke so's they would die quicker. And sure 'nuff, the soldiers come and broke both fellers legs on either side a Jesus. Then they come to Jesus and seen that he was already dead so they did'n break none a his legs. But, one of 'em stuck 'eem in the side with a spear and blood and water come out. This here's a true, eyewitness report y'all, given to ye so that ye might just up and believe. This stuff happened so's the good book could come true where it says, "Nary a one of 'ees bones'll be broke" and "They's gonna be seein' the one they stuck".

King Jesus, The Comeback Special!

By and By, ole Joseph from Arimathea come ferward and asked Pilate if he could take Jesus' body down. He was a secret follower a

89

Jesus cuz he was kindly skeert a the religious folk. So, sure 'nuff, he come and got the body. Ole Nicodemus showed up again too. He was the feller that had come by at night before. He brought with 'eem a mess a high falutin' spices and myrhh and aloe and such, purt near seventy-five pounds worth, so's they could kindly embalm 'eem. Them two fellers took the body and wrapped it up with the spices in a gret big cloth, 'cuz that was kindly the way the Jews used to bury folks. Just a short piece away they was a brand new tomb in a garden that had'n never been used. Cuz it was gettin' to be time fer the Passover and since that there tomb was so close that's where they laid 'eem down.

Early Sundee mornin', 'fore the first light even, Mary Magdalene come over to the tomb and seen that the big ole rock door a the tomb had plumb been rolled off. She run off and hunted up Rocky and the disciple that Jesus shore did love alot and says to 'em, "They done run off with the Lord's body and I don't have no idee where they could a took 'eem!"

Rocky and the other disciple run off like scalded dawgs to the tomb to see what was up. The other feller put it in overdrive, though, and got their first. He hunkered down and looked in and seen the cloth sittin' there but, did'n go inside. But when ole Rocky got there, 'course he just barreled right in. He seen all the grave clothes sittin' there and the cloth that had been around 'ees head was folded up, purdy as ye please, off to the side. Then the other disciple come in and when he seen it he just up and believed. 'Fore that time they really did'n git the fact that accordin' to the good book, He was gonna come back to life.

Then the two fellers went on home, but Mary stayed behind, just a ballin', and whilst she cried, she hunkered down and looked inside. Then she saw two angels, dressed up all shiny and white, a sittin' on the place where Jesus had laid, one at the head and one at the foot. And they says, "Why ye ballin', hun?"

She blubbered out, "Cuz they done took my Lord, and I ain't got no idee what they done with 'eem." Then she kindly looked over her shoulder and seen Jesus standin' there, but she did'n know it was him.

"Why ye ballin', hun?" he says. "Who ye lookin' fer?"

She kindly reckoned he was the gardener or somethin' so she says, "Sir, if'n ye took 'eem off, just tell me where ye put 'eem, and I'll go fetch 'eem."

"Mary!" Jesus says.

And she turned and looked square at 'eem and says, "Rabbi!"

"Don't hug my neck, hun, cuz I ain't gone up to the Daddy yet.

But run tell my bros that I'm fixin'to go up to see my Daddy and yer

Daddy, to see my God and yer God.

Mary hunted up the disciples and hollared, "I done seen the

Lord!" Then she kindly told 'em what he said.

Ole Doubtin' Thomas Gits to Worshippin'

That night they was meetin' with all the doors locked up tight,

cuz they was skeert a the Jewish religious big shots. All the sudden

Jesus come and stood right there in their midst and says, "Shalom,

Peace be with y'all!" Onced he'd spoke he held out 'ees hands fer 'em

to see and showed 'em 'ees side. And they was plumb beside

themselves with joy to see their Lord again! He says to 'em again,

"Peace be with y'all, now. Just like the Daddy sent me, I'm sendin'

y'all." Then he blowed on 'em and says, "I won't y'all to have the

Holy Spirit. If'n y'all fergive folks sins, they's fergiven, if'n ye don't,

they ain't."

Now ole Thomas (we called 'eem The Twin) wud'n with 'em

that time that Jesus come. But they told 'eem bout it, "We done seen

92

the Lord!" And he says, "I ain't a gonna believe it less'n I see where they poked the nails in 'ees hands and touch it, and stick my hand in there where they stuck 'eem in the side."

Eight days after that, they was together again and this time ole Thomas was there too. All the doors was locked, but all the sudden, just like before, Jesus just popped in. "Shalom! Peace be with y'all!" Then he says to Thomas, "Kindly stick yer finger on my hands there. Kindly stick yer hand in my side. Now, quit yer doubtin' and just up and believe!"

"Yer my Lord and yer my God too!" Thomas hollared out.

Then Jesus says to 'eem, "Ye believed it cuz ye seen it fer yerself. Bless them folks that ain't gonna see it, but up and believe anyway."

Jesus disciples seen 'eem do a whole bunch a mir'cles that ain't even in this here book. But these here are wrote down so's y'all would up and believe that Jesus is the King, the Son a God, and that on account yer believin', ye might have the good life and keep on livin' it ferever and ever.

After while, Jesus popped up again by the Sea a Galilee. This here's how it come about. A bunch a the disciples was there, they was Rocky and Thomas (we called 'eem The Twin), Nathaneal from Cana over in Galilee, Zebedee's boys, and another two.

Rocky up and says, "I'm a goin' fishin', y'all."

"Wait up, we's goin' too!" they all says. So off they go in the boat, but did'n catch nary a fish all night long. Come mornin' time they saw Jesus standin' over yonder on the beach, but they did'n know it was him. He hollared out, "Hey good buddies, y'all ketch anything yet?"

"Naw", they says.

Then he says, "Thow yer net yonder on the right-hand side and yer sure to ketch a mess a fish!" So they done just that and they could'n even haul 'em all in they caught so many.

Right then the disciple that Jesus shore did love a lot says to Rocky, "Hey, it's the Lord!" When Rocky heard that he thowed 'ees robe on (cuz he had taken it off to work) and just up and dove in the water just a breast strokin' it to beat the band til' he got to shore. The other fellers brung the boat back, cuz they was only out 'bout three hunnerd feet out. When they come to shore, they seen they was a barbecue goin' and fish a fryin' and bread to eat too.

"Bring some a them there fish y'all just caught" Jesus says. So Rocky went and drug the net up and they was a hunnerd and fifty-three whoppers in there, but the net did'n even tear.

"Now, y'all come git ye some vittles fer breakfast" Jesus says. Nobody asked 'eem if'n he really was the Lord cuz they all knew fer sure it was him. Then Jesus commenced to servin' em up a breakfast a fish and bread. This here was the third time he popped up since he come back from the dead.

After they'd done et, Jesus says to Rocky, "Simon, do ye really love me more than these here fellers?"

Rocky says, "Sure 'nuff, Lord. Ye know I love ye"

"Then I won't ye to feed my little lambs, ah ight."

Then Jesus says it again. "Simon, do ye love me?"

"Sure 'nuff, Lord. Ye know I love ye", says Rocky.

"Then I won't ye to take special care a my sheep", says Jesus.

One more time he says, "Simon, son a John, do ye love me."

Rocky kindly got 'ees feelin's hurt then and he says, "Aw Lord, ye know ever'thang. Ye know good and well I love ye."

Jesus says, "Then I won't ye to feed my sheep. Sure 'nuff, when ye was young ye done whatever ye won'ted to and just up and went when ye got good and ready, but when ye git old some fellers is gonna take ye by the hand and take ye where ye don't really wanna go. Jesus says that so's he'd kindly know what kind a death he was gonna have to go through to show God's shininess. Then Jesus up and says, "Foller after me!"

Rocky turned 'round and seen the disciple Jesus shore did love a comin' after 'em. This here was the same one that leaned over at supper and says, "Lord, reckon who's gonna be the turncoat?" So Rocky asked 'eem, "Well, what about that feller there, Lord?"

Jesus replied, "Well, I reckon it ain't nunna yer b'ness if'n I just up and says 'ees gonna live 'til I git back. Yer b'ness is to foller me." So, there kindly spread a rumor that this here feller wud'n never gonna die, but Jesus wud'n really sayin' that. He was just sayin' "If I up and says 'ees gonna live 'til I git back."

Now, that there disciple and the one that's tellin' this here story, y'all...well, they's one and the same. And ever' single on of us will tell ye the same thing, cuz it's the truth. And ye know what? I did'n even tell y'all the half of it. I reckon if'n I told all of it, they'd be a mess a

books so big the whole world would'n even hold 'em all.

Afterwerd, Evangelism and Such

The main purpose a this here little book was to kindly interduce y'all to King Jesus. Now I reckon I'd be remiss if'n I did'n give y'all a chance to ask 'eem into yer heart. What this means is ye just admit ye done sinned and ask 'eem to come into yer heart and help ye to kindly do better. He don't physic'ly come into yer heart, that might cause a blockage. It's all spiritual stuff. But, if'n ye won't to, I reckon it might go somethin' like this here:

Lord, fergive me. I knowed I done wrong and I thankee kindly fer payin' the price fer my sins. I'm gonna just up and believe that ye died on the cross fer me and that ye was raised on the third day too. Now, please come on in here and kindly clean up the place.

If'n ye prayed that there prayer I'd love to hear from ye. This here King Jesus won't let ye down atol. He'll come in just like he said he would and you'll know it sure 'nuff, next time ye git to wantin' to misbehave and there's a little voice that says, "Huh, uh, that ain't you no more, Buddy Roe!." That there's King Jesus talking to ye, y'all!

Commence to findin' ye a good church where they love on ye quite a bit and where the preacher kindly puts ye in mind a King Jesus with 'ees kindness, and patience, love, and joy and such. Talk to King Jesus and tell 'eem what ye need and what's botherin' ye and what not! That there's called prayer. But ain't no reason fer it to be high-falutin', it's just talkin' and listenin' to King Jesus. And read yer Bible cuz it's God's love letter to ye.

Aw, I almost fergot. The way this thing works is I tell you and then you go tell somebody and then they go tell somebody and so on and so forth. So if'n this here book blessed yer heart and the rest a ye, please do me a favor and git ye a mess a Hillbilly Bibles and just up and give 'em away. They don't cost much. Now, don't take grandmaw's bunyion surgery money, y'all! Just do it if'n ye can swing it and all. This here's the good news y'all... so SPREAD IT LIKE PEANUT BUTTER!!!

Bless your heart and all the rest a ye,

Stevie Rey

hillbillybible@gmail.com

www.myspace.com/hillbillybible

To Order a Mess a Hillbilly Bibles So's Ye Can

Up and Give 'em Away

If'n y'all won't to order a whole mess a Hillbilly Bibles, I commend ye fer it and ask the good Lord to please bless ye. Now, ye may be wonderin' how much is a "mess" a Hillbilly bibles? Well, that's fer y'all to decide.

When my Nanny used to go out in the truck patch and git a "mess" a turnip greens or a "mess" a polk salad she'd brang it in and we'd have it fer dinner (That there's lunch fer my yank pals). But it was always a good little bit, 'nuff to fill ye up.

Fer some folks a "mess" might be to up just give way one Hillbilly Bible, and that's just fine and dandy my dear heart. Don't ye feel a bit guilty 'bout it if'n that's all ye can do. Fer some folks the good Lord has blessed yer socks off, and a "mess" is gonna be enough Hillbilly Bibles to wallpaper that there Tagma Hall. I ain't gonna tell ye how much is a "mess." Pray about it. God'll tell ye.

Now, who do I won't ye to give 'em to. Ever'body, y'all! Give 'em to some a these high-falutin', uppity atheists. Give 'em to churches, fer to give out to the community. Give 'em to homeless folks. Give 'em to religious folks (some of them's the one's that needs it the most, y'all). Give 'em to the rich, give 'em to the poor, give 'em to black folks and white folks, and red folks, and more!

Ah ight. I reckon I done started to sound like Dr. Suess, so I'll wind it up, but y'all git the point don't ye? This here's the good news.

SPREAD IT LIKE PEANUT BUTTER, Y'ALL!

This here's where ye order 'em.

http://stores.lulu.com/hillbillybible

Love y'all,

Stevie Rey

Q) Why did you decide to do The Hillbilly Bible?

A) Well, 1) I'm southern. 2) I like The Bible. 3) I reckon there's reason to believe that Jesus and probably most a the disciples did, in fact, speak with a country accent, y'all!

After a little while, those standing there went up to Peter and said, "Surely you are one of them, for your accent gives you away." Matthew 26:73 [NIV]

Q) What purpose does The Hillbilly Bible serve?

A) Well, y'all, my vision is that this little book will be used as an evangelism tool, much like one'd use a tract. Secondarily, my prayer is that perhaps it will help folks that is already Christians git to know King Jesus a little better.

Q) Are you a trained theologian?

A) Well, naw, not hardly. I have me a little preacher trainin' and a whole lot a personal Bible study, but no academic credentials in the field a theology. But, lemme say this, I'd druther be taught by a spirit-filled dummy than a edgy-cated legalist anyday. Y'all know what a legalist is don't ye? That there's a feller that'll run over a homeless man to git to church on time. Religious folk...like them there Fairy-sees back yonder that conspired to kill our Lord.

Q) So, what makes you think you are qualified for such an undertaking?

A) Grace. Folks, please understand. The Hillbilly Bible ain't no study Bible. It is what it is- kind of a fun way to introduce people to the gospel and maybe give a little insight into King Jesus, 'ees sense a humor, 'ees teachin's, and 'ees message, and maybe most of all 'ees relationships- especially 'ees relationship to 'ees Daddy. Cuz, that there relationship He had with 'ees Daddy, y'all. That's how He won'ts it to be fer us and our heavenly Daddy.

Q) Do you plan on doing any other books of the Bible in "hillbilly"?

A) Well, I ain't opposed to it. I'd kindly like to do Galatians, Romans, Proverbs, and Psalms...mayhaps some others...we'll just have to wait and see how thangs go.

Q) Do you really talk like that?

A) Hee, hee. Why shore, hun. Don't ever'body in the south talk like this?

Q) How do you go about rendering a verse into "hillbilly"?

A) Well, the first thang I done was to read several diff'ernt versions a the verse, NIV, KJV, NKJV, and NLT to get a good feel for what is actually bein' said. Then I give 'er a go. If'n I'm havin' a particularly hard time with a verse I'll sort a pray my way thew it, and a course, I'm in a lot of just general daily prayer 'bout it anyway. I pray all the time, y'all. I'm real spir'tual like that....quit laughin', y'all!

Well, thank y'all again, fer readin' The Hillbilly Bible, I'll talk to ye next time around...and remember...

King Jesus Loves Ye and Stevie Rey Loves Ye too!

Stevie

Printed in the United States
132409LV00008B/129/P

9 780615 179254